FOREWORD BY

the MIRACLE MORNING

FOR SALESPEOPLE

THE FASTEST WAY TO TAKE YOUR SELF AND YOUR SALES TO THE NEXT LEVEL

HAL ELROD | RYAN SNOW

WITH HONORÉE CORDER

THE MIRACLE MORNING FOR SALESPEOPLE
Hal Elrod

Interior Design: Garrett Robinson, LookLikeABestseller.com

WHAT OTHER SALES EXPERTS ARE SAYING...

"Hal Elrod is more than an inspiration. He has taken his incredible story and turned it into lessons that you can use to create your own miracles."

—Jeffrey Gitomer, NY Times Bestselling Author, *The Sales Bible*

"If you're looking for the new way to improve your sales and effectiveness it's time to look inward and change what you are actually doing with your day - literally first thing in the morning. It might sound simple but this book has the power to turn your sales and your life around!"

—Andrea Waltz, Co-author of *Go for No!*

"Having trained salespeople in over 45 countries, and ranked in the World's Top 10 Sales Gurus since 2008, it is great to see what Hal Elrod and Ryan Snow have done with *The Miracle Morning for Salespeople.* In sales, and in life, time is your most valuable asset. Jump-start your day by investing morning time in the most important person in the world, and when you make this a daily discipline, watch your sales soar with velocity.

—Bob Urichuck, Velocity Selling Specialist and author of *Velocity Selling*

"Hal Elrod & Ryan Snow have hit a HOME RUN with their book *The Miracle Morning for Salespeople!* If you want to get your day off to GREAT start apply what they teach in this book!"

—Eric Lofholm, author of *21 Ways to Close More Sales Now*

"Hal Elrod and Ryan Snow have created a movement that will transform America's salespeople. Up early and armed with profoundly simple, but not-so-obvious truths, *The Miracle Morning for Salespeople* will impact sales in every industry in a way not seen since Og Mandino's *The Greatest Salesman in the world*. Buy this in bulk and give to your sales team and your friends, because it's no fun to be rich and successful by yourself!"

—**Tom Schaff, author of** *Big Swift Kick*

"I LOVE this book… Hal Elrod and Ryan Snow have created a book that every salesperson needs to read, and every sales manager needs to get in the hands of every person on their team, to give them the best chance of succeeding. Highly recommended.

—**David Osborn, author of** *Wealth Can't Wait* **and founder one of the top real estate brokerages in the world with $4.5 billion per year in sales**

A SPECIAL MESSAGE FROM ROBERT KIYOSAKI, AUTHOR OF *RICH DAD POOR DAD*

"Hal Elrod is a genius, and his book *The Miracle Morning* has been magical in my life.

"I have been in the *human potential / personal development movement* since 1973, when I did my first EST training and saw a whole new world of possibilities. Since then, I have studied religions, prayer, meditation, yoga, affirmation, visualization, and NLP (neuro-linguistic programming). I've walked on fire and explored other 'unconventional' philosophies, some 'too far out there' to mention.

"What Hal has done with his acronym SAVERS is take the best practices—developed over centuries of human consciousness development—and condensed the 'best of the best' into a daily morning ritual. A ritual that is now part of my day.

"Many people do *one* of the SAVERS daily. For example, many people do the *E*, they *exercise,* every morning. Others do *S* for *silence* or meditation, or *S* for *scribing* or journaling. But until Hal packaged SAVERS no one was doing all six ancient 'best practices' every morning.

"*The Miracle Morning* is perfect for very busy, successful people. Going through SAVERS every morning is like pumping rocket fuel into my body, mind, and spirit... *before* I start my day, every day.

"As my rich dad often said, 'I can always make another dollar, but I cannot make another day.' If you want to maximize every day of your life, read *The Miracle Morning.*"

A Special Invitation from Hal

Fans and readers of *The Miracle Morning* make up an extraordinary community of like-minded individuals who wake up each day, dedicated to fulfilling the unlimited potential that is within all of us. As creator of *The Miracle Morning*, it was my responsibility to create an online space where readers and fans could go to connect, get encouragement, share best practices, support one another, discuss the book, post videos, find an accountability partner, and even swap smoothie recipes and exercise routines.

I honestly had no idea that **The Miracle Morning Community** would become one of the most inspiring, engaged, and supportive online communities in the world, but it has. I'm blown away by the caliber of our 16,000+ members, which consists of people from all around the globe, and is growing daily.

Just go to **www.MyTMMCommunity.com** and request to join The Miracle Morning Community (on Facebook). Here you'll be able to connect with like-minded individuals who are already practicing *The Miracle Morning*—many of whom have been doing it for years—to get additional support and accelerate your success.

I'll be moderating the Community and checking in regularly. I look forward to seeing you there!

If you'd like to connect with me personally on social media, follow **@HalElrod** on Twitter and **Facebook.com/YoPalHal** on Facebook. Please feel free to send me a direct message, leave a comment, or ask me a question. I do my best to answer every single one, so let's connect soon!

DEDICATION

HAL

This book is dedicated to the leadership at Vector Marketing and Cutco Cutlery for giving me the opportunity to develop the mindset and selling skills that have enabled me to achieve everything I've ever wanted. Please keep developing leaders and changing lives.

Also, to the most important people in my life—my family. My loving and supportive wife, Ursula, and our two children, Sophie and Halsten. I love you all more than I can put into words.

RYAN

I am thankful to my family for their support while I put countless hours into researching and writing this book. Special thanks to my wife, Mary Lynn, who has done a wonderful job raising our three beautiful, smart, and amazing children, Connor, Lily, and Harrison. Every day would be less of a miracle without all of you in my life. Thank you for pushing me to write this book and share it with the world.

CONTENTS

FOREWORD
BY TODD DUNCAN

I have always believed that the truest measure of your success is invisible to your prospects and clients. It's below the surface of your skin, hidden in the depths of your soul, and it is yearning and in most cases, pleading, to come alive.

What I know for certain is that success is always, one hundred percent of the time, first and foremost, an inside game. You have undoubtedly heard the phrase, "pour your heart into it." If you take that seriously, you have the one thing you need to be more successful than you have ever dreamed. It's the heart, your heart, which creates the motivation that is necessary to bring your dreams alive. It fuels your belief, fires your passion, and unlocks your potential.

Hal Elrod and Ryan Snow have masterfully crafted the "how to" on this truth in *The Miracle Morning for Salespeople*. From the very first word to the last, they lay down truth after truth on how you can get ALL the success you have ever dreamed of and, in the process, achieve the deepest levels of significance you could ever hope for.

Last year I had the good fortune of having Hal Elrod on our Sales Mastery stage, and as he impacted the crowd, and shared stories like Ryan's, you I knew immediately there was something special about his message. Every day, each day, you get a chance to decide the kind of day you are going to have. You can let it be overwhelmed with chaos, confusion, uncertainty, excuses, and drama, or you can make it magical, memorable, and filled with certainty, belief, passion, and purpose. Yes, you can decide to make today your *Masterpiece*. It is your choice. That decision, beyond any decision, will set in motion the circumstances for you to achieve the greatness God has gifted you to experience. And I believe the morning is where that miracle happens.

The secret of a winning life, which includes a productive and purposeful sales career, has and will always be based on your character. The process of getting the life and career you want is found in the principles of integrity, honesty, dignity, contribution, faith, repetition, patience, quality, excellence, effort, and service. *The Miracle Morning for Salespeople* unpacks each of these traits with compelling stories, fast-paced and actionable ideas, and believable solutions that will cascade over and impact every area of your life.

Having taught millions of salespeople success principles, I'm seeing in Hal and Ryan a fresh voice with a unique approach to an age-old trade. This book will appeal to common sense as it presents a systematic game plan that will satisfy your heart's desire. It's a total-person approach to life and sales, and touches all the bases that are "musts" if you're going to enjoy the balanced success all of us dream about.

It's good stuff!

Todd Duncan
CEO, The Duncan Group
NY Times Bestselling Author of *Time Traps, High Trust Selling, The $6,000 Egg*

INTRODUCTION
MY MIRACLE MORNING

"Salesmen are made—not born. If I did it, you can do it."

—JOE GIRARD, the World's Greatest Salesman
as listed in the Guinness Book of World Records

I*'m just going to press the snooze button, one more time...*

That was how every morning used to begin for me. In fact, *snooze* isn't just the button that used to start my day, it was also the best way to describe my whole *career*. That was *before The Miracle Morning*. I was stuck in a job that didn't challenge me with a paycheck that didn't inspire me. I went from day to day with no clear path for the future and few prospects for change. It seemed like my entire life was set for *snooze*.

But few people would have sensed my dissatisfaction. From the outside, I looked successful. My family lived in an 1,800 square foot apartment with a huge yard. We were planning to buy a home. My wife and I both held college degrees and were earning $40,000–$50,000 a year, placing us firmly in the middle class. We were, to the casual observer, just a happy American family.

On the inside, though, I felt anything but happy. I dragged myself out of bed each morning. I felt powerless, lethargic, and unfulfilled. Worse still, I knew in my heart that the only person to blame was *me*. I had been playing small and safe, and I was dissatisfied with the results.

I wanted more. My family deserved more. I was sure I could *have* more. The problem was that I didn't know what to do. I felt I needed a miracle.

And, thankfully, I got one.

My Miracle Morning

Hal Elrod, my co-author and friend, I met over a decade ago when we were both working for the same company. Hal was a Hall of Fame sales representative, and I was one of the top new branch managers. We lived on opposite coasts and didn't work together directly, but I had seen Hal speak at numerous conferences.

When I took a break from sales to dive into my passion for teaching, which is what I had wanted to do when I left college, I followed Hal online. I watched him leave a six-year career as a top salesperson and shift towards coaching, speaking, and writing. I read and loved his first book, *Taking Life Head On*, and I eventually hired Hal to be my coach.

I tell you all of this because I can remember several years ago when Hal started posting video blogs about getting out of bed at 4:00 a.m. and going for a run. As the director of the *Run for the Front* charity event, to raise money for the Front Row Foundation, I remember hearing Hal talk about his training for his ultra-marathon. I recall his confidence and excitement. I was uplifted by his passion and power. So, when Hal announced that he was launching another book, I wanted to read it. I volunteered to read the book before the launch and to help share the book with others when it came out.

I have to admit that wasn't pure altruism on my part. At this point, I had found my way back into sales. I was still teaching, but had started a new career in real estate. With a wife, two kids, and two jobs, there was very little time for me to work on developing myself personally or as a salesperson. Hal's new book, *The Miracle Morning*, was more than a nice idea. It was a necessity.

I read it in a day.

It was one of the best books I had ever read. The next day, when I started my first Miracle Morning 30-Day Challenge, it just clicked. I was excited to get out of bed that morning.

And the next.

And the next.

And then I started to notice changes. Small at first. Then huge. My whole life, morning by morning, literally *transformed.*

In the three years since reading *The Miracle Morning*, there have been so many improvements in my life I could not possibly list them all here, but these are a few that make me the most proud:

- I have left my teaching job and grown my real estate business to a point where I have quadrupled my income in the last three years.

- I was awarded the Rookie of the Year Award by both my Keller Williams office and by the North Shore Association of Realtors for my success in sales.

- I was able to take charge of my financial situation, create a budget, and find multiple ways to increase my income.

- I went from taking less than three listings in my first year, to taking three listings in one day.

- I have read over 35 books and listened to an additional 25 books in the car as well as countless hours of podcasts.

- I have drastically transformed my circle of influence in business.

- I have written my first book, and I have already started working on my second.

- I have been hired as a team leader/business coach for an office of 85 real estate agents.

- I manage a leveraged real estate sales team without managing the day-to-day operations.

The Miracle Morning helped me create a set of habits to remove the internal and external barriers that were holding me back. For the first time, I feel as though I am in complete control of both the direction and velocity of my personal and professional life. And the results prove it. It took me over 30 years to earn a $100,000 in a year. **It took me less than two years to double that number once I got there.**

That was my miracle. Now it's time for yours.

The Miracle Morning for Salespeople

My story was the initial inspiration for this book. Hal watched me transform my life from the ground up, going back into sales and making more and more sales and money than ever before, taking my relationship to a new level, dramatically expanding my network, improving my health, and becoming truly happy in the process.

And I'm not the only one. Since Hal started sharing *The Miracle Morning*, initially with his clients and then with many others upon the release of the book, the success stories have poured in. They all sounded incredibly similar. Each person had been either experiencing tremendous challenges, or simply not succeeding to their full potential, then discovered *The Miracle Morning* and the *Life S.A.V.E.R.S.*, and turned things around in record time:

I was failing, miserable, and considering a career change. My brother gave me The Miracle Morning, *and within sixty days, I had risen from last place to first place in my office.*

I sold $127,000 worth of Cutco Cutlery in my first three years. Then I heard about The Miracle Morning *and Hal's* Life S.A.V.E.R.S., *and began using them right away. Now, in just the first five months of this year, I've sold more than $400,000 worth of these awesome knives! Thanks, Hal!*

I'm living life at a Level 10 every single day. Not only have my sales doubled and then doubled again, I've lost 40 pounds, started a side business, and bought a new house and the car of my dreams. I'm so thankful I found The Miracle Morning!

There were hundreds more, and they kept arriving almost daily. Hal and I noticed, however, that the first *Miracle Morning* book struck a chord with many salespeople in particular. People began to ask for *Miracle Morning* techniques specific to improve sales (and many other topics), and we began to wonder: *could we do more?*

We knew there were countless books written for salespeople about techniques, prospecting, generating leads, building rapport, handling objections, closing the sale, collecting referrals, and following up to generate repeat business.

We also knew there were a plethora of books that share the secrets of the happiest and most productive people on the planet. Books upon books that delved into how to be content, thrilled, creative, imaginative, inspired, resourceful, dynamic, magnetic, energetic, self-motivated, and unendingly ambitious.

But what we thought salespeople needed more than anything was *both*. Not just strategies for how to be a selling machine, but also a daily practice to become the most joyful, incredible, and fulfilled version of themselves.

In writing this book, we invested over two years interviewing dozens of top salespeople—including CEOs, entrepreneurs, business owners, and bestselling authors—who were each in the top 1 percent of their respective companies or fields. We wanted to find out what they did differently from the other 99 percent, and you'll learn what we discovered in the chapters to come. The average income of these individuals ranged from a quarter million to multi-seven figures, and while much of what we found surprised us, just as much did not.

The more you study the world's top salespeople in any industry, the more you realize that their success is a result of *who they are,* not just what they do. We've written this book because we want you to have both—to simultaneously master every aspect of successful selling while you master every facet of *yourself.*

And therein lies the premise, and promise of this book: **If you want to take your SALES to the next level, you must first figure out how to take your SELF to the next level—***because it only happens in that order.*

If you want to attract, create, and sustain extraordinary levels of success, sales, and income, you must first figure out how to become the person that is capable of easily and consistently attracting, creating, and sustaining the extraordinary levels of success, sales, and income that you desire.

Then, you must master what the top salespeople know about selling. You need to learn the intricacies and nuances of the sales process—things like pre-sale preparation, prospecting, approaching prospects, presenting, demonstrating, handling objections, and, finally, closing the sale.

The Miracle Morning for Salespeople is not your grandfather's sales book. It's the twenty-first century answer to a twenty-first century challenge: how to succeed in *every* area of your life simultaneously and how to be a top seller *and* experience a life of health, balance, and fulfillment. This is a book that tells you what the top salespeople do, and it gives you an edge, right from the very beginning, by helping you to become one of them—mentally, emotionally, spiritually, *and* strategically.

It's Your Turn

What if you could wake up tomorrow morning with absolute faith the day was going to be awesome? What if waking up early was a habit you absolutely loved? What if every morning could be like Christmas morning—you know, the really awesome Christmas mornings of your childhood? When you went to bed full of anticipation of what was going to happen the next day, and woke up so excited you awakened your parents at 4:00 a.m. to get on with the business of ripping open all of your gifts. (Or was that just me?) Any interest?

I can assure you that's exactly how I feel each and every day. I go to bed looking forward to the next day and wake up each morning *before my alarm goes off* because I can't wait to see what miracles the day holds for me. Almost every day is better than the day before. I can't believe my life has transformed into something so amazing.

I know—you might be thinking, *I've tried and failed. I've tried to get up earlier. I've tried to master my life and my sales. I have failed more times than I care to admit, and I'm nervous about trying something new. Can this really help me?*

Yes! Yes! *Yes!*

I've been on both sides of the coin. I know what it's like to struggle to meet my sales quotas, and I know what it's like to succeed beyond my wildest dreams. Even writing this book wouldn't have crossed my mind a few short years ago.

I know what it's like to search for greener grass, and I know what it's like to have the lawn that my colleagues and competitors envy and causes them to ask me for my secret sauce. This book *is* my secret sauce. I've included every single distinction, action, and hack I use to stay at the top of my sales game ... and my life, too.

More importantly, I believe you're ready. Ready to take yourself, your sales, and your life to levels that, deep down, you know you're capable of, *or you wouldn't be reading this book.* The principles within this book can be the means to realize your dreams and to start earning more money than you ever have before—the kind of money that will allow you to move beyond the stress that inconsistent sales and mediocre paychecks cause and into a life and career that supports the life you've always dreamed of living.

I believe that to be truly successful, in whatever way *you* measure success, you must master both your inner game and the outer game of sales. And that starts in the morning. When you own the morning, you own the day. When you own the day, you can own the sales process. When that happens, *you own the sale.* I know that, because it was possible for me to do it, it is just as possible for you to do it, too.

If you let it, *The Miracle Morning for Salespeople* can be your coach, accountability partner, and mastermind team all rolled into one. I want it to be your constant companion until your sales career has been so completely transformed that you can't recognize where you started. Keep this book and your journal close at hand so you can reference it, make notes, jot down the distinctions you make, and track your progress.

You can be just as successful, if not more so, than I have been. You can take the success I've enjoyed and multiply it for yourself.

All you have to do to start is take control of your morning.

Are you ready?

— 1 —
WHY MORNINGS MATTER
(MORE THAN YOU THINK)

"True success doesn't begin with the stuff on the outside—whom you persuaded last week, how much you sold last month, what you earned last year, or how much you can afford to buy this year. Lasting success is built with the stuff on the inside—who you are and who you want to become, why you sell, and what legacy you intend to leave."
—TODD DUNCAN, NY Times bestselling author, High Trust Selling

How you start each morning sets your mindset, and the context, for the rest of your day. Start every day with a purposeful, disciplined, growth-infused, and goal-oriented morning, and you're virtually guaranteed to crush your day.

Yet most salespeople start their days with procrastination, hitting the snooze button, and sending a message to their subconscious that says they don't even have enough self-discipline to get out of bed in the morning, let alone do what's necessary to reach their sales goals.

When the alarm clock starts beeping in the morning, consider it to be akin to life's first gift to us. It's the gift of time to dedicate to becoming the person you need to be to achieve all of your goals and dreams while the rest of the world is still asleep.

You might be thinking, *All of this sounds great, Ryan. But. I. Am. Not. A. Morning. Person.*

I understand, I really do! You're not saying anything I haven't told myself a thousand times before. And believe me, I tried—and failed—many times to take control of my mornings. But that was before I discovered *The Miracle Morning.*

Stay with me for a minute. In addition to having more sales than you can count without a fancy calculator and making more money than you can manage with a snazzy investment advisor, I bet you also want to stop struggling, end worrying about having more month than money, quit missing your sales quotas, and release all of the intense and not-so-great emotions that go along with those challenges. Right?

Then know this:

Mornings are the key to all of it.

It's a *fact* supported by tons of evidence that early risers tend to be happier, make more money, and *produce more sales* than individuals who get a late or sluggish start to their day.

But, before we get into exactly *how* you can master your mornings, let me make the case for *why*. Because believe me, once you know the truth about mornings, you'll never want to miss one again.

Why Mornings Matter So Much

I mentioned facts and scientific evidence, and there's plenty. The more you dig into mornings, the more the proof mounts that the early bird gets a *lot* more than the worm. Here are just a few of the key advantages to laying off the snooze button:

You'll be more proactive. Christoph Randler is a professor of biology at the University of Education in Heidelberg, Germany.

In the July 2010 issue of *Harvard Business Review*, Randler found that "People whose performance peaks in the morning are better positioned for career success, because they're more proactive than people who are at their best in the evening."

You'll anticipate problems and head them off at the pass. Randler went on to surmise that morning people hold all of the important cards. They are "better able to anticipate and minimize problems, are proactive, have greater professional success and ultimately make higher wages." He noted that morning people are able to anticipate problems and handle them with grace and ease, which makes them better in business ... and, *ahem*, sales.

You'll plan like a pro. Morning folks have the time to organize, anticipate, and plan for their day. Our sleepy counterparts are reactive rather than proactive, leaving a lot to chance. Aren't you more stressed when you sleep through your alarm or when you wake up late in general? Getting up with the sun (or before) lets you get a jump-start on the day. While everyone else is running around trying (and failing) to get their day under control, you'll be calm, cool, and collected.

You'll have more energy. One of the components of your new *Miracle Mornings* will be morning exercise, which—in as little as just a few minutes a day—sets a positive tone for the day. Increased blood to the brain will help you think more clearly and focus on what's most important. Fresh oxygen will permeate every cell in your body and increase your energy all day, which is why top salespeople who exercise report being in a better mood and in better shape, getting better sleep, and being more productive. This, of course, will result in you producing significant increases in your sales numbers.

You'll gain early bird attitude advantages... Recently, researchers at the University of Barcelona in Spain, compared morning people, those early birds who like to get up at dawn, with evening people, night owls who prefer to stay up late and sleep in. Among the differences they found is that morning people tend to be more persistent and resistant to fatigue, frustration, and difficulties. That translates into lower levels of anxiety and lower rates of depression, higher life satisfaction, and less likelihood of substance abuse. Sounds good to me.

...and you'll avoid night owl disadvantages. On the other hand, evening people tend to be more extravagant, temperamental, impulsive, and novelty-seeking, "with a higher tendency to explore the unknown." They are more likely to suffer from insomnia and ADHD. They also appear to be more likely to develop addictive behaviors, mental disorders, and antisocial tendencies and even to attempt suicide. Not a pretty picture.

If a biologist, the University of Barcelona, and the Harvard Business Review aren't enough to convince you to give the power of early rising and *The Miracle Morning* a chance, I don't know what will.

The evidence is in, and the experts have had their say. *Mornings contain the secret to an extraordinarily successful sales future.*

Mornings? Really?

I'll admit it. To go from *"I'm not a morning person"* to *"I really want to become a morning person"* to *"I'm up early every morning, and it's pretty flippin' amazing!"* is a process. But after some trial and error, you will discover how to out-fox, pre-empt, and foil your inner late sleeper so you can make early rising a habit.

Okay, sounds great in theory, but you might be shaking your head and telling yourself, *There's no way. I'm already cramming twenty-seven hours of stuff into twenty-four hours. How on earth could I get up an hour earlier than I already do?* I ask the question, "How can you not?"

The key thing to understand is that *The Miracle Morning* isn't about trying to deny yourself another hour of sleep so you can have an even longer, harder day. It's not even about waking up earlier. It's about waking up *better*.

Thousands of people around the planet are already living their own *Miracle Mornings*. Many of them were night owls. But they're making it work. In fact, they're *thriving*. And it's not because they simply added an hour to their day. It's because they added *the right* hour. And so can you.

Still skeptical? Then believe this: **The hardest part about getting up an hour earlier is the first five minutes**. That's the moment in which—tucked into your warm bed—you re-make the decision as to whether you start your day or hit the snooze button *just one more time*. It's the moment of truth, and the decision you make right then will change your day, your sales, and your life.

And that's why that first five minutes is our starting point for *The Miracle Morning for Salespeople*. It's time for you to win every morning!

In the next two chapters, we'll make waking up early easier and more exciting than it's ever been in your life (even if you've *never* considered yourself to be a morning person), and we'll show you how to maximize those newfound morning minutes.

Chapters 4, 5, and 6 will reveal not-so-obvious selling principles related to accelerating your personal growth, why you need to strategically engineer your life for endless amounts of energy, and how to optimize your ability to stay focused on your goals and what matters most.

Finally, chapters 7, 8, and 9 cover the sales acceleration skills you must master to elevate your sales career and increase your income as fast as humanly possible.

We have a lot of ground to cover in this book, so let's jump right in!

TOP ONE PERCENT SALESPERSON INTERVIEW
Bob Urichuck – CEO, Velocity Selling
Specialist, and author, *Velocity Selling*

Bob's giving attitude and desire to share with others make him stand out from a crowd even more so than his sales prowess. Bob adopted a village in Sri Lanka and has been responsible for the medical care and education of over 700 children who survived the tsunami. Bob has worked in several capacities in sales over the last 50 years, starting in a family business when he was only six. Bob has been ranked number four in the world's top 30 sales gurus (2012) and has maintained a top eight ranking since 2008.

Bob was kind enough to share with us his morning routine and a couple of his favorite sales success tips: "I am a morning person, s0 I dedicate a minimum of one hour of my most productive time to the most important person in the world—myself. I wake up at 6 a.m. After stretching I meditate, first by visualizing helping someone else in need and then by visualizing my ultimate goal. When that is done, I listen to my affirmations that I created on my iPhone for about 25 minutes. Then I reward myself with my first cup of coffee and give thanks for being able to have a cup of coffee when there are millions of people around the world who cannot get a clean glass of water. I am thankful. Then I exercise—a 6 km walk or a 50 lap swim, and then I reward myself with breakfast, and my day begins."

I wanted to share three tips that stuck with me from Bob's interview:

1. Believe in yourself, the organization you represent, its products and services, and the team you work with.

2. Sales is not about making a sale; it's about creating a relationship. The more relationships you have, the bigger your network. The bigger your network, the bigger your net worth.

3. In sales, 70 percent of the time you are listening, and 30 percent of the time you are asking questions, which means there is no time for talking. It's not about you, your product or service,

or your brand. It's all about the buyer, and when you are buyer focused, you facilitate the buying process and empower them to buy.

MIRACLE MORNING SUCCESS STORY

Stephen Christopher – CEO, Seequs Marketing
Technologies

Before I read *The Miracle Morning*, my life was GO, GO, GO, but I often ended each day feeling that I didn't accomplish enough, and I felt guilty when going to bed because I should have done more. Then I woke up, already stressed about all the things that I needed to do, and hit the snooze button at least one to three times each morning, hoping that another 15 minutes of sleep would help solve my problems.

After the first full day of *The Miracle Morning*, I kept waking up at night hoping that it was time to get out of bed and start my day... I was so excited that I could hardly sleep!

Within the first four days of doing *The Miracle Morning*, I brought in at least one new lead per day, and within the first ten days I closed four new clients (*My track record high was about four to five per month, which is already great in the industry).

The amount of focus and clarity that *The Miracle Morning* has helped me to create is unbelievable. I get four times as much accomplished every day, I feel so much happier at the end of the day because I know I took the right actions and helped other people get closer to accomplishing their goals in life.

I believe so much in *The Miracle Morning* that I already ordered 60 copies of the book and I can't wait to pass them out to friends, colleagues, and anyone that I meet that just needs a little help. In 10 days, my girlfriend and close friends have seen such a difference in me that five of them have already started *TMM* as well!

Thanks to Hal, *The Miracle Morning* has changed my life, and now I am on track to have a Miracle Life!

— 2 —
IT ONLY TAKES FIVE MINUTES TO BECOME A MORNING PERSON

If you really think about it, hitting the snooze button in the morning doesn't even make sense. It's like saying, "I hate getting up in the morning, so I do it over, and over, and over again."
—DEMETRI MARTIN, Stand-up Comedian

It is possible to love waking up—even if you've *never* been a morning person.

I know you might not believe it. Right now you think, *That might be true for early birds, but trust me, I've tried. I'm just not a morning person.*

But it's true. I know, because I've been there. I was a bleary-eyed, snooze-button pusher. A "snooze-aholic" as Hal calls it. I was a morning dreader. I hated waking up.

And now I love it.

How did I do it? When people ask me how I transformed myself into a morning person—and transformed my life in the process—I tell them I did it in five simple steps, one step at a time. I know it may seem downright impossible. But take it from a former snooze-aholic: you can do this. And you can do it the same way that I did.

That's the critical message about waking up—it's possible to change. Morning people aren't born—they're self-made. You can become a morning person, and you can do it in simple steps that don't require the willpower of an Olympic marathoner. I contend that, when early rising becomes not something you do but *who you are*, you will truly love mornings. Waking up will become for you, like it is for me, effortless.

Not convinced? Suspend your disbelief just a little and let me introduce you to the five-step process that changed my life. Five simple, snooze-proof keys that make waking up in the morning—even early in the morning—easier than ever before. Without this strategy, I would still be sleeping (or snoozing) through my alarm(s) each morning. Worse, I would still be clinging to the limiting belief that I was not a morning person.

And I would have missed a whole world of opportunity.

The Challenge with Waking Up

Waking up earlier is a bit like trying a new diet: It's easy to get pumped up about all the great results you're going to get, starting tomorrow.

But when tomorrow comes? And you're hungry? And your favorite food is staring up at you from the fridge or the café menu?

Well … we all know what happens then. Good intentions flee the building. Motivation goes into hibernation. And the next thing you know, you're curled up with a tub of ice cream.

Mornings are not so different. Right now, I bet you're plenty motivated. But what happens tomorrow morning when that alarm goes off? How motivated will you be when you're yanked out of a deep sleep in a warm bed by a screaming alarm clock in a cold house?

I think we both know where motivation will be right then. It will have gone off-shift and been replaced by rationalization. And rationalization is a crafty master—in just seconds we can convince ourselves that we just need a few extra minutes…

…and the next thing we know we're scrambling around the house late for work. Again.

It's a tricky problem. Just when we need our motivation the most—those first few moments of the day—is precisely when we seem to have the least amount of it.

The solution, then, is to boost that morning motivation. To mount a surprise attack on rationalization. That's what the five steps that follow do. Each step in the process is designed to do one thing: increase what I call your Wake-Up Motivation Level (WUML).

Right now, you might have a low WUML, meaning you want nothing more than to go back to sleep when your alarm goes off. That's normal. But by using this process, you can reach a high WUML, where you're ready to jump up and embrace the day.

The Five-Minute Snooze-Proof Wake-Up Strategy

Minute One: Set Your Intentions Before Bed

The first key to waking up is to remember this: Your first thought in the morning is usually the last thought you had before you went to bed. I bet, for example, that you've had nights where you could hardly fall asleep because you were so excited about waking up the next morning. Whether it was Christmas Eve or the night before a big vacation, as soon as the alarm clock sounded you opened your eyes ready to jump out of bed and embrace the day. Why? It's because the last thought you had about the coming morning before you went to bed was positive.

On the other hand, if your last thought before bed was something like, *Oh man, I can't believe I have to get up in six hours—I'm going to be exhausted in the morning!* then your first thought when the alarm clock goes off is likely to be something like, *Oh my gosh, it's already been six hours?? Nooo! I just want to keep sleeping!*

The first step, then, is to consciously decide every night to actively and mindfully create a positive expectation for the next morning.

For help on this and to get the precise words to say before bed to create your powerful intentions, download *The Miracle Morning Bedtime Affirmations* free at www.TMMBook.com.

Minute Two: Move Your Alarm Clock Across the Room

If you haven't already, move your alarm clock across the room. This forces you to get out of bed and engage your body in movement. Motion creates energy—when you get all the way up and out of bed, it naturally helps you wake up.

If you keep your alarm clock next to your bed, you're still in a partial sleep state when the alarm goes off, and it makes it much more difficult to wake yourself up. In fact, you may have turned off the alarm without even realizing it! On more than a few occasions, you might even have convinced yourself that your alarm clock was merely part of the dream you were having. (You're not alone on that one, trust me.)

Simply forcing yourself to get out of bed to turn off the alarm clock will instantly increase your WUML. However, you'll still likely be feeling more sleepy than not. So to raise that WUML just a little further, try…

Minute Three: Brush Your Teeth

As soon as you've gotten out of bed and turned off your alarm clock, go directly to the bathroom sink to brush your teeth. While you're at it, splash some water on your face. This simple activity will increase your WUML even further.

Now that your mouth is fresh, it's time to…

Minute Four: Drink a Full Glass of Water

It's crucial that you hydrate yourself first thing every morning. After six to eight hours without water, you'll be mildly dehydrated, and dehydration causes fatigue. Often when people feel tired—at any time of the day—what they really need is more water, not more sleep.

Start by getting a glass or bottle of water (or you can do what I do, and fill it up the night before so it's already there for you in the morning), and drink it as fast as is comfortable for you. The objective is to replace the water you were deprived of during the hours you slept. (And hey, the side benefits of morning hydration are better, younger-looking skin and even maintaining a healthy weight. Not bad for a few ounces of water!)

That glass of water should raise your WUML another notch, which will get you to….

Minute Five: Get Dressed or Jump in the Shower

The fifth step has two options. Option #1 is to get dressed in your exercise clothes, so you're ready to leave your bedroom and immediately engage in your *Miracle Morning*. You can either lay out your clothes before you go to bed or even sleep in your workout clothes. (Yes, really.)

Option #2 is to jump in the shower. I usually change into exercise clothes, since I'll need a shower after, but a lot of people prefer the morning shower because it helps them wake up and gives them a fresh start to the day. The choice is yours.

Regardless of which option you choose, by the time you've executed these five simple steps, your WUML should be high enough that it requires very little discipline to stay awake for your *Miracle Morning*.

If you were to try and make that commitment at the moment your alarm clock first went off—while you were at a WUML of nearly zero—it would be a much more difficult decision to make. The five steps let you build momentum so that within just a few minutes you're ready to go instead of still sound asleep.

Miracle Morning Bonus Wake-Up Tips

Although this strategy has worked for thousands of people, these five steps are not the only way to make waking up in the morning easier. Here are a few other tips I've heard from fellow Miracle Morning practitioners:

- *The Miracle Morning Bedtime Affirmations*: If you haven't done this yet, be sure to take a moment now to go to www.TMMbook.com and download the re-energizing, intention-setting *Miracle Morning Bedtime Affirmations*, for free. There is nothing more effective for ensuring you will wake up before your alarm than programming your mind for exactly what you want.

- Set a timer for your bedroom lights: One of *The Miracle Morning Community* members sets his bedroom lights on a timer (you can buy an appliance timer online or at your local hardware store.) As his alarm goes off, the lights come on in the room. What a great idea! It's a lot easier to fall back asleep when it's dark—having the lights on tells your mind and body that it's time to wake up. (Regardless of whether or not you use a timer, be sure to turn your light on first thing when your alarm goes off.)

- Set a timer for your bedroom heater: Another fan of *The Miracle Morning* says that in the winter, she keeps a bedroom heater on an appliance timer set to go off fifteen minutes before she wakes up. She keeps it cold at night, but warm for waking up so that she won't be tempted to crawl back under her covers!

Feel free to add to or customize the *Five-Minute Snooze-Proof Wake-Up Strategy*, and if you have any tips you're open to sharing, we'd love to hear them. Please share them in **The Miracle Morning Community** at www.MyTMMCommunity.com.

Waking up consistently and easily is all about having an effective, pre-determined, step-by-step strategy to increase your WUML in the morning. Don't wait to try this! Start tonight by reading *The Miracle Morning Bedtime Affirmations*, moving your alarm clock across the room, setting a glass of water on your nightstand, and committing to the other two steps for the morning.

How to Go From Unbearable to Unstoppable (In 30 Days)

Incorporating any new habit requires an adjustment period—don't expect this to be effortless from day one. But stick with it. The seemingly unbearable first few days are only temporary. While there's a lot of debate around how long it takes to create a new habit, thirty days is definitely enough to test-drive your new morning routine.

Here's what you might expect as you build your new routine:

Phase One: Unbearable (Days 1–10)

Phase One is when any new activity requires tremendous effort, and getting up early is no different. You're fighting existing habits, the very habits that have often been entrenched in *who you are* for years.

In this phase, it's mind over matter—and if you don't mind, it'll definitely matter! The habits of hitting snooze and not making the most of your day are the same habits that are holding you back from becoming the superstar salesperson you have always known you can be, so dig in and hold strong.

In Phase One, you're fighting existing patterns and limiting beliefs. But it's also where you find out what you're made of and what you're capable of. You need to keep pushing, stay committed to your vision, and hang in there. Trust me when I say you can do this!

Phase Two: Uncomfortable (Days 11–20)

In Phase Two, your body and mind begin to become acclimated to waking up earlier. You'll notice getting up earlier starts to get a tiny bit easier, but it's not yet a habit—it's not quite who you are and likely won't yet feel natural.

The biggest temptation at this level is to reward yourself by taking a break, especially on the weekends. A question posted quite often in The Miracle Morning Community is, "How many days a week do you get up early for your Miracle Morning?" My answer—and the one that's most common from long-time Miracle Morning practitioners… *every single day.*

Once you've made it through Phase One, you've made it through the hardest period. So keep going! Why on earth would you want to go through that first phase again by taking one or two days off? Trust me, you wouldn't, so don't!

Phase Three: Unstoppable (Days 21–30)

Phase Three is where the magic happens! Early rising is now not only a habit, it has literally become part of *who you are*. Part of your identity. Your body and mind will have acclimated to your new way of being. These next 10 days are important for cementing the habit into yourself and your life.

As you engage in *The Miracle Morning* practice, you will also develop an appreciation for the three distinct phases of habit change. A side benefit is you will realize you can identify, develop, and adopt any habit that serves you—up to and including the habits of the top performers I have included in this book!

I know it can be daunting on day five to realize you still have 25 days to go before your transformation is complete and you've become a bona fide morning person. Keep in mind that on day five, you're actually already half way through the first phase and well on your way. Keep your eye on the prize, your vision clear in your mind, and the words you think and say carefully selected to encourage you on your journey. Remember: your initial feelings are not going to last forever. In fact, you owe it to yourself to persevere because in no time at all, you'll be getting the exact results you want as you become the person you've always wanted to be!

What Do I DO With My Morning?

Thirty days, you might be thinking. *I can get up earlier for thirty days…. But what do I DO with that time?*

This is where the magic begins. I'm going to introduce you to the routines at the heart of *The Miracle Morning*. They're called the Life S.A.V.E.R.S., and they're the habits that are going to transform your mornings, your sales, and your life!

Taking Immediate Action:

There's no need to wait to get started with creating your new, amazing future. As Anthony Robbins has said, "When is NOW a good time for you to do that?" Now, indeed, would be perfect! In fact, the sooner you start, the sooner you'll begin to see results, including increased energy, a better attitude, and, of course, more sales.

Step 1: Set your alarm for one hour earlier than you usually wake up, and schedule that hour in your calendar to do your first *Miracle Morning* … tomorrow morning.

From this day forward, starting with the next 30 days, keep your alarm set for 60 minutes earlier to start waking up when you *want* to, instead of when you *have* to. It's time to start launching into each day with a *Miracle Morning* so that you can become the person you need to be to take yourself, your sales, and your success to extraordinary levels.

What will you do with that hour? We're going to find out in the next chapter, but for now, simply continue reading this book during your *Miracle Morning* until you learn the whole routine.

Step 2: Join The Miracle Morning Community at www.MyT-MMCommunity.com to connect with and get additional support from more than 15,000 like-minded early risers, many of whom have been generating extraordinary results with *The Miracle Morning* for years.

Step 3: Find a *Miracle Morning* accountability partner. Enroll someone—a friend, family member, or colleague—to join you on this adventure and hold each other accountable to follow through until *The Miracle Morning* has become a lifelong habit.

TOP ONE PERCENT SALESPERSON INTERVIEW

Corey Ackerman – Senior Partner, Cornerstone
Search Group

After obtaining a law degree and opening and selling several successful businesses with his brother, Corey has spent the last 12 years propelling himself to the top one percent of sales in his firm in the recruiting business. Corey prides himself on becoming a nationally and internationally recognized expert in a key area of recruiting in the pharmaceutical industry.

Corey offers a plethora of sales tips, but his number one tip is this: "You should always go into every encounter with your customers with an idea of what success will look like, and try to achieve that. So, even if you think you are unlikely to make the sale, then use the encounter as an opportunity to build the relationship for the future, or try a new approach. All in all, always figure out in advance what a positive outcome would be and try to achieve that."

In discussing his morning routine, Corey describes his method of visualizing his daily activities. "When I take a shower or during my ride to work, I figure out what success will look like for my most important work activities that day and think of how I can achieve those successes. I also practice conversations I'm going to have, thinking of the hardest questions I'm going to be asked and actually answer them. I actually speak the answers out loud as I find I always sound better in my head than I sound when I actually speak it aloud."

MIRACLE MORNING SUCCESS STORY
Lorie VanWerden – Owner, Fruitful Sales &
Development

"Being in sales and hearing "NO" many times on a daily basis is tough—but now, with some of the direction from *The Miracle Morning,* I feel like I am more UP, HOPE-FILLED and ENTHU-SIASTIC about my work and my life.

I work for myself, by myself, alone, in my house all day, so it's hard to stay focused and UP without a support group around me. Doing *The Miracle Morning* and listening to Hal's podcast (and taking in his energy) helps me stay positive and live a life of balance and fulfillment. I would say that I have always been a pretty positive person, but since knowing Hal and reading his books and listening to his podcasts I feel like I am getting the added direction and extra push I needed to achieve my goals.

I made up a vision board (which I would have never done before *The Miracle Morning,* and I was able to secure some meetings with some pretty large accounts, which was very exciting! I attribute part of being able to get those meetings was directly related to practicing the Visualization and also the Affirmations. You are what you think about and what you put into your mind so since TMM I have even more 'good stuff' going in and when you put the 'good' in you are bound to get 'good out!'

Plus I love sharing *The Miracle Morning* with other people—helping them to be the best that they can be too and encouraging them in this journey called life!"

THE LIFE S.A.V.E.R.S.

SIX PRACTICES GUARANTEED TO SAVE YOU FROM A LIFE OF UNFULFILLED POTENTIAL

*"What Hal has done with his acronym S.A.V.E.R.S. is taken the best practices—developed over centuries of human consciousness development—and condensed the best of the best into a daily morning ritual. A ritual that is now part of my day. Many people do one of the SAVERS daily. For example, many people do the **E**, they exercise every morning. Others do **S** for silence or meditation, or **S** for scribing or journaling. But until Hal packaged SAVERS, no one was doing all six ancient best practices every morning. The Miracle Morning is perfect for very busy, successful people. Going through SAVERS every morning is like pumping rocket fuel into my body, mind, and spirit... before I start my day, every day."*
—ROBERT KIYOSAKI, best-selling author,
Rich Dad, Poor Dad

When Hal was experiencing the second of his two self-proclaimed rock bottoms, both of which you can read about in *The Miracle Morning*, he began his own quest for the fastest way to take his personal development to the next level. So, he went in search of the daily practices of the world's most successful people.

After discovering six of the most proven, timeless personal development practices, Hal first attempted to determine which one or two would accelerate his success the fastest. Then he had a realization: *What would happen if I did ALL of them?*

Hal and I have been friends for well over a decade, and I saw firsthand his total transformation after discovering, implementing, and mastering those practices, which he came to call the Life S.A.V.E.R.S.

To my astonishment, Hal changed almost overnight. But it wasn't just him. I watched countless others adopt the Life S.A.V.E.R.S. and transform themselves, too. And I soon followed.

Why the Life S.A.V.E.R.S. Work

The Life S.A.V.E.R.S. are simple but profoundly effective daily morning practices to help you plan and live your life on your terms. They're designed to start your day in a peak physical, mental, emotional, and spiritual state so that you are both constantly improving and will ALWAYS perform at your best.

I know, I know. You don't have time. You probably feel like you can barely squeeze in what you have to do already, never mind what you want to. But I "didn't have time" either. And yet, here I am, with more time, and more prosperity, than I've ever had.

What you need to realize right now is that the *Miracle Morning* is what creates time for you. The Life S.A.V.E.R.S. are the vehicle to help you stop working harder and longer and begin working smarter and more efficiently instead. The practices help you build energy, see priorities more clearly, and help you find the stress-free productive flow in your life.

In other words, the Life S.A.V.E.R.S. don't take more time from your day but ultimately add more to it.

Each letter in S.A.V.E.R.S. represents one of the best practices of the most successful salespeople on the planet. And they're also the same activities that bring new levels of peace, clarity, motivation, and energy to your life. They are:

Silence

Affirmations

Visualization

Exercise

Reading

Scribing

These practices are the best possible use of your newfound morning time. They're customizable to fit you, your life, and your goals. And you can start first thing tomorrow morning.

Let's go through each of the six practices in detail.

S is for Silence

Silence, the first practice of the Life S.A.V.E.R.S., is a key habit for salespeople. If you're surrounded by the endless barrage of phone calls, emails, sales meetings, cold calls, tracking sheets, and pending deals that make up a life in sales, this is your opportunity to STOP and BREATHE!

Most salespeople start the day by checking email, texts, and sales numbers on their smart phones. And most people struggle with sales. It's not a coincidence. Starting each day with a period of silence instead will immediately reduce your stress levels and help you begin the day with the kind of calm and clarity that you need in order to focus on what's most important.

Many of the most successful people in sales, but also in all professions, are daily practitioners of silence. It's not surprising that Oprah practices stillness—or that she does nearly all of the other Life S.A.V.E.R.S., too. Musicians Katy Perry and Russell Brand practice TM (transcendental meditation) as do Sheryl Crow and Sir Paul McCartney. Film and television stars Jennifer Aniston, Ellen Degeneres, Cameron Diaz, Clint Eastwood, and Hugh Jackman have all spoken of their daily meditation practice. Even famous billionaires Ray Dalio and Rupert Murdoch have credited their *financial* success to practicing stillness on a daily basis. You'll be in good (and quiet) company by doing the same.

If it seems like I'm asking you to simply do nothing, let me clarify: you have a number of choices for how to build your practice of silence. In no particular order, here are a few to get you started:

- Meditation
- Prayer
- Reflection
- Deep breathing
- Gratitude

Whichever you choose, be sure you don't stay in bed for your period of silence, and better still, get out of your bedroom altogether. I sit on my living room couch, where I already have everything set up that I need for my *Miracle Morning*: affirmations, journal, yoga DVD, and the books I'm currently reading. It's all set up the night before, so it's easy to jump right in and engage in my *Miracle Morning* the moment I wake up.

The Benefits of Silence

How many times as salespeople do we find ourselves in stressful situations? How many times are we dealing with immediate obstacles that take us away from our vision or plan? No, those aren't trick questions—the answer is the same for both: every single day. Stress is one of the most common reasons that salespeople lose focus and lose business. I'm often faced with the ever-present distractions of other people encroaching on my schedule and the inevitable fires of the day. Quieting the mind allows me to put those things aside and focus on working *on* my business instead of *in* it.

But the effect goes beyond productivity. Excessive stress is terrible for your health, too. It triggers your fight or flight response, and that releases a cascade of toxic hormones that can stay in your body for days. That's fine if you only experience that type of stress occasionally. But when the constant barrage of a life in sales keeps the adrenaline flowing all the time, the negative impact on your health adds up.

Silence in the form of meditation, however, can reduce stress, and as result, improve your health. A major study run by several groups including The National Institutes of Health, the American Medical Association, the Mayo Clinic, and scientists from both Harvard and Stanford have stated that meditation can reduce stress and high blood pressure. A recent study by Dr. Norman Rosenthal, a world-renowned psychiatrist who works with the David Lynch Foundation, even found that people who practice meditation are 30 percent less likely to die from heart disease.

Practicing silence, in other words, can help you reduce your stress and replace medication with meditation at the same time.

Guided Meditations and Meditation Apps

Meditation is like anything else—if you've never done it before, then it can be difficult or feel awkward at first. If you are a first time meditator, I recommend starting with a guided meditation.

Here are a few of our favorite meditation apps that are available for both iPhone/iPad and Android devices:

- Headspace
- Omvana
- Simply Being

There are both subtle and significant differences among these meditation apps, one of which is the voice of the person speaking.

If you don't have a device that allows you to download apps, simply go to YouTube or Google and search on the keywords "Guided Meditation."

Miracle Morning (Individual) Meditation

When you're ready to try an unguided meditation, here is a simple, step-by-step meditation you can use during your *Miracle Morning*, even if you've never meditated before.

- Before beginning your meditation, it's important to prepare your mindset and set your expectations. This is a time for you to quiet your mind and let go of the compulsive need to constantly be thinking about something—reliving the past or worrying about the future, but never living fully in the present. This is the time to let go of your stresses, take a break from worrying about your problems, and be fully present in this moment. It is a time to access the essence of who you truly are—to go deeper than what you have, what you do, or the labels you've accepted as who you are. If this sounds foreign to you, or too new age, that's okay. I've felt the same way. It's probably only because you've never tried it before. But thankfully, you're about to.

- Find a quiet, comfortable place to sit. You can sit up straight on the couch, on a chair, on the floor, or on a pillow for added comfort.

- Sit upright, cross-legged. You can close your eyes, or you can look down at a point on the ground about two feet in front of you.

- Begin by focusing on your breath, taking slow, deep breaths. Breathe in through the nose and out through the mouth. The most effective breathing should cause your belly to expand and not your chest.

- Now start pacing your breath; breathe in slowly for a count of three seconds (one one thousand, two one thousand, three one thousand), hold it in for another three counts, and then breathe out slowly for a final count of three. Feel your thoughts and emotions settling down as you focus on your breath. Be aware that, as you attempt to quiet your mind, thoughts will still come in to pay a visit. Simply acknowledge them, and then let them go, always returning your focus to your breath.

- Try being fully present in this moment. This is often referred to as just being. Not thinking, not doing, just being. Continue to follow your breath, and imagine inhaling positive, loving and peaceful energy, and exhaling all of your worries and stress. Enjoy the quiet. Enjoy the moment. Just breathe… Just be.

- If you find that you have a constant influx of thoughts, it may be helpful for you to focus on a single word, phrase, or mantra and repeat it over and over again to yourself as you inhale and exhale. For example, you might try something like this: (On the inhale) "I inhale confidence…" (As you exhale) "I exhale fear…" You can swap the word confidence with whatever you feel like you need to bring more of into your life (love, faith, energy, etc.), and swap the word fear with whatever you feel like you need to let go of (stress, worry, resentment, etc.).

Meditation is a gift you can give yourself every day. My time spent meditating has become one of my favorite parts of my routine. It's a time to be at peace and to experience gratitude and freedom from our day-to-day stressors and worries.

Think of daily meditation as a temporary vacation from your problems. While your problems will still be there when you finish your daily meditation, you'll find that you're much more centered, and better equipped to solve them.

A is for Affirmations

Have you ever wondered why some of the top salespeople around you regularly surpass even your best sales month? Or why others selling the same thing can only sell enough to scrape by? Time and time again, it is a salesperson's *mindset* that shows up as the driving factor in sales performance.

From prospective clients to colleagues, those around you can sense your mindset. It shows up undeniably in your language, your confidence, and your demeanor. And as a result, your attitude affects the entire sales process, from opening conversations to closing deals. Show me a great salesperson, and I'll show you someone with a great mindset.

I know firsthand, though, how difficult it can be for salespeople to maintain confidence and enthusiasm—not to mention motivation—during the rollercoaster ride of the sales cycle. Mindset is largely something we adopt without conscious thought—at a subconscious level, we have all been programmed to think, believe, act, and talk to ourselves a certain way. When times get tough, we revert to our habitual, programmed mindset.

Our programming has come from many influences, including what we've have been told by others, what we've told ourselves, and all of our good and bad life experiences. That programming expresses itself throughout your life, including in your sales performance. And that means if you want better sales, you need better mental programming.

Affirmations are a tool for doing just that. By repeatedly telling yourself who you want to be, what you want to accomplish, and how you are going to accomplish it, your subconscious mind will shift your beliefs and behavior. You'll automatically believe and act in new ways, and eventually manifest your affirmations into your reality.

Science has proven that affirmations—when done correctly—are one of the most effective tools for quickly becoming the person you need to be to achieve everything you want in your life. And yet, affirmations also have a bad rap. Many have tried them only to be disappointed, with little or no results.

Why the Old Way of Doing Affirmations Doesn't Work

For decades, countless so-called experts and gurus have taught affirmations in ways that have proven to be ineffective and set you up for failure, time and time again. Here are two of the most common problems with affirmations.

Lying to Yourself Doesn't Work

I am a millionaire. No, you're not.

I have 7% body fat. No, you don't.

I have achieved all of my goals this year. Nope. Sorry, you haven't.

This method of creating affirmations that are written as if you've already become or achieved something may be the single biggest reason that affirmations haven't worked for most people.

With this technique, every time you recite an affirmation that simply isn't rooted in truth, your subconscious will resist it. As an intelligent human being who isn't delusional, lying to yourself repeatedly will never be the optimum strategy. *The truth will always prevail.*

Passive Language Doesn't Produce Results

Many affirmations have been designed to make you feel good by creating an empty promise of something you desire. For example, here is a popular money affirmation that's been perpetuated for decades, by many world-famous gurus:

I am a money magnet. Money flows to me effortlessly and in abundance.

This type of affirmation might make you feel good in the moment by giving you a false sense of relief from your financial worries, but it won't generate any income. People who sit back and wait for money to magically show up are cash poor.

In order to generate financial abundance (or any result you desire, for that matter), you've got to actually do something. Your actions must be in alignment with your desired results, and your affirmations must articulate and affirm both.

4 Steps to Create Affirmations That Increase Sales

Here are simple steps for creating and implementing results-oriented *Miracle Morning* affirmations, which will program both your conscious and subconscious mind to produce results and take your levels of personal and professional success beyond what you've ever experienced before.

Step 1: The Extraordinary Result You Are Committed to and Why

Notice we're not starting with "What you want." Everyone wants things, but we don't get what we want; we get what we're committed to. You want to be a millionaire? Who cares; join the nonexclusive club. Oh wait, you're 100 percent committed to becoming a millionaire by clarifying and executing the necessary actions until the result is achieved? Okay, now we're talking.

Action: Start by writing down a (specific) extraordinary result/ outcome—one that challenges you and would significantly improve your life—which you are ready to commit to creating (even if you're not yet sure how you will do it). Then, reinforce your commitment by including your WHY—the compelling benefits that you'll get to experience.

Examples: *I am committed to doubling my income in the next 12 months, from $_____ to $_____, so that I can provide financial security for my family.*

Or…

I am 100% committed to losing _____ pounds and weighing _____ pounds by _____ (date) so that I have more energy and set an example of health and fitness for my kids.

Step 2: The Necessary Actions You Are Committed to Taking and When

Writing an affirmation that merely affirms what you want without affirming what you are committed to doing is one step above pointless and can actually be counter-productive by tricking your subconscious mind into thinking that the result will happen automatically, without effort.

Action: Clarify the (specific) action, activity, or habit that is required for you to achieve your ideal outcome, and clearly state WHEN and how often you will execute the necessary action.

Examples: To guarantee that I double my income, I am committed to doubling my daily prospecting calls from 20 to 40 calls five days a week from 8:00 a.m. to 9:00 a.m.—NO MATTER WHAT.

Or

To ensure that I lose _____ pounds, I am 100 percent committed to going to the gym 5 days per week and running on the treadmill for a minimum of 20 minutes each day from 6:00 a.m. to 7:00 a.m.

The more specific your actions are, the better. Be sure to include frequency (how often), quantity (how many), and precise time frames (which times you will begin and end your activities).

Step 3: Recite Your Affirmations Every Morning with Emotion

Remember, your *Miracle Morning* affirmations aren't designed to merely make you *feel good*. These are written statements that are strategically engineered to program your subconscious mind with the beliefs and overall mindset you need to achieve your desired outcomes, while directing your conscious mind to keep you focused on your highest priorities and taking the actions that will get you there.

However, in order for your affirmations to be effective, it is important that you tap into your emotions while reciting them. Mindlessly repeating an affirmation over and over again, without intentionally feeling its truth, will have minimal impact for you. You must take responsibility for generating authentic emotions, such as excitement and determination, and powerfully infusing those emotions into every affirmation you recite.

Action: Schedule time each day to read your affirmations in the morning (ideally during your *Miracle Morning*), to both program your subconscious and focus your conscious mind on what's most important to you and what you are committed to doing to make it your reality. That's right, you must read them daily. Reading an occasional affirmation is as effective as getting an occasional workout. You'll start seeing results only once you've made them a part of your daily routine.

Step 4: Constantly Update and Evolve Your Affirmations

As you continue to grow, improve, and evolve, so should your affirmations. When you come up with a new goal, dream, or any extraordinary result that you want to create for your life, add it to your affirmations.

Personally, I have affirmations for every single significant area of my life (finances, health, happiness, relationships, parenting, etc.) and am constantly updating my affirmations as I learn more. And I am always on the lookout for quotes, strategies, and philosophies that I can add to improve my mindset. Any time you come across an empowering quote or philosophy and think to yourself, *Man, that is a huge area of improvement for me*, add it to your affirmations.

Your programming can be changed and improved at any time, starting right now. You can reprogram any perceived limitations with new beliefs and behaviors so you can become as successful as you want to be, in any area of life you choose.

In summary, your new affirmations will articulate which extraordinary results you are committed to creating, why they are critically important to you, and most importantly, which necessary actions you are committed to taking, and precisely when you are committed to taking them to ensure that you attain and sustain the extraordinary levels of success that you truly want (and deserve) for your life.

Affirmations to Become a Top Salesperson

In addition to the formula to create your affirmations, I have included this list of sample affirmations, which are regularly used by top salespeople to increase sales and productivity and to improve in different areas of their business. Feel free to include any of these that resonate with you:

- I am just as worthy, deserving, and capable of achieving extraordinary success as any other person, and I will prove it today with my actions.

- I am destined for greatness, and today I will live in alignment with my destiny.

- Selling isn't about me and what I want; it is about connecting with my prospect by finding out what's important to them, and then matching my product to meet their wants and needs.

- Remember that people buy based on emotion and how they feel, so my job isn't to convince a prospect that they "can't live without" my product. It's to paint a compelling picture (through words and stories) that gets them emotionally en-

gaged in the experience of owning my product. I will make it
fun and exciting for them to buy!

- The secret to success in selling is to be committed to my daily
process without being emotionally attached to my results. I
can't always control my daily results, but as long as I follow
through with the process, the law of averages will *always* play
out, and my results will take care of themselves.

- I commit to making a minimum of ___ prospecting calls, Mon-
day through Friday between ___:___ AM/PM and ___:___
AM/PM, no matter what.

- I view my clients and prospects as valued friends, and by focusing on how I can selflessly add value to their lives, I will
become a trusted advisor to them.

- Because I always seek to add value for every person I meet, my
clients gladly refer me to their contacts. So, I confidently ask
for and get 5–10 referrals from every one of customers.

- I believe in my products, and I have the utmost confidence
that I can help my clients to solve problems, and make their
life/work better.

- I provide a high level of customer service and ensure my clients
are satisfied.

- I respond to emails and phone calls within 24 hours.

- I focus on learning new things and improving my sales skills
daily, and I commit to reading at least one or two new books
every month.

- I continue to develop knowledge about my product, and I read
industry news weekly to stay ahead of my competition.

- Negativity will not stand in my way. I maintain a positive
mindset and look for the good in every situation.

- I increase my sales every month because I am committed to
constant and never-ending improvement.

- I dedicate time each week to nurturing my relationships with
my clients, and I generate tons of repeat business.

These are just a few examples of affirmations. You can use any of these that resonate with you, or create your own affirmations using the four-step formula taught in the previous pages. Anything you repeat to yourself, over and over again, with emotion will be programmed into your subconscious mind, form new beliefs, and manifest itself through your actions.

V is for Visualization

Visualization is a technique for using your imagination to create what you want in life.

Visualization is a well-known habit of top performing athletes, who use it to enhance their performance. What is less well known is that successful salespeople, the top achievers, use it just as frequently.

What Do You Visualize?

Most salespeople are limited by visions of their past results, replaying previous failures and heartbreaks. Creative visualization, on the other hand, enables you to design the vision that will occupy your mind, ensuring that the greatest pull on you is your future—a compelling, exciting, and limitless future.

Here's a brief summary of how I use visualization, followed by three simple steps you can use to create your own visualization process.

After I've read my affirmations, I sit upright, close my eyes, and take a few slow, deep breaths. For the next five to ten minutes, I simply visualize my long term goals becoming a reality, then visualize myself living my ideal day, performing all tasks with ease, confidence, and enjoyment.

For example, during the months that I spent writing this book, I would first visualize the end result—people reading the finished book, loving it, and telling their friends about it. Then I visualized writing with ease, enjoying the creative process, free from stress, fear, and writer's block. Visualizing the process as enjoyable, and free from stress and fear motivated me to take action and overcome procrastination. And now, you hold the results of that visualization in your hands today. Pretty cool, right?

In sales, you can visualize success in the short-term, too. Picture yourself having conversations with prospects during morning phone calls. Spend time imagining your presentation with your new client. What does it look like? How does it feel as you develop a great relationship? Imagine yourself solving a problem for your client. Picture yourself answering objections and questions. Envisioning success will prepare you for, and almost ensure, a successful day.

3 Simple Steps for Miracle Morning Visualization

Directly after reading your affirmations is the perfect time to visualize yourself living in alignment with your affirmations.

Step 1: Get Ready

Some people like to play instrumental music in the background—such as classical or baroque (check out anything from the composer J.S. Bach)—during their visualization. If you'd like to experiment with playing music, put it on with the volume relatively low.

Now, sit up tall in a comfortable position. This can be on a chair, the couch, or the floor. Breathe deeply. Close your eyes, clear your mind, and get ready to visualize.

Step 2: Visualize What You Really Want

The greatest gift you can give to the people you love is to live up to your full potential. What does that look like for you? What do you really want? Forget about logic, limits, and being practical. If you could have anything you wanted, do anything you wanted, and be anything you wanted, what would you have? What would you do? What would you be?

Visualize your major goals, deepest desires, and most exciting, would-totally-change-my-life-if-I-achieved-them dreams. See, feel, hear, touch, taste, and smell every detail of your vision. Involve all of your senses to maximize the effectiveness of your visualization.

The more vivid you make your vision, the more compelled you'll be to take the necessary actions to make it a reality.

Fast forward into the future to see yourself achieving your ideal outcomes and results. You can either look toward the near future—the end of the day—or further into the future, like I did while writing this book. See yourself accomplishing what you set out to accomplish, and experience how good it will feel to have followed through and achieved your goals.

Step 3: Visualize Who You Need To Be and What You Need To Do

Once you've created a clear mental picture of what you want, begin to visualize yourself living in total alignment with the person you need to be to achieve your vision. See yourself engaged in the positive actions you'll need to do each day (exercising, studying, working, writing, making calls, sending emails, etc.) and make sure you see yourself enjoying the process. See yourself smiling as you're running on that treadmill, filled with a sense of pride for your self-discipline to follow through.

Picture the look of determination on your face as you confidently, persistently make those phone calls, work on that report, or finally take action and make progress on that project you've been putting off for far too long. Visualize your co-workers, customers, family, friends, and spouse responding to your positive demeanor and optimistic outlook.

Final Thoughts on Visualization

In addition to reading your affirmations every morning, daily visualization will turbocharge the programming of your subconscious mind for success. You will begin to live in alignment with your ideal vision and make it a reality.

Visualizing your goals and dreams is believed by some experts to attract your visions into your life. When you visualize what you want, you stir up emotions that lift your spirits and pull you toward your vision. The more vividly you see what you want, and the more intensely you allow yourself to experience now the feelings you will feel once you've achieved your goal, the more you make the possibility of achieving it feel real.

When you visualize daily, you align your thoughts and feelings with your vision. This makes it easier to maintain the motivation you need to continue taking the necessary actions. Visualization can be a powerful aid to overcoming self-limiting habits, such as procrastination, and to taking the actions necessary to achieve your goals.

E is for Exercise

Exercise should be a staple of your *Miracle Morning*. Even a few minutes of exercise each morning significantly enhances your health, improves your self-confidence and emotional well being, and enables you to think better and concentrate longer. You'll also notice how quickly your energy level increases with daily exercise, and your clients will notice it, too—even over the phone.

Personal development experts and self-made multi-millionaire entrepreneurs Eben Pagan and Anthony Robbins (who is also a bestselling author) both agree that the number one key to success is to "start every morning off with a personal success ritual." Included in both of their success rituals is some type of morning exercise. If it's good enough for Eben and Tony, it's good enough for me!

Lest you think you have to engage in triathlon or marathon training, think again. Your morning exercise also doesn't need to replace an afternoon or evening regimen, if you already have one in place. You can still hit the gym after your sales calls. However, the benefits from adding as little as five minutes of morning exercise are undeniable, including improved blood pressure and blood sugar levels, and decreased risk of all kinds of scary things like heart disease, osteoporosis, cancer, and diabetes. Maybe most importantly, a little exercise in the morning will increase your energy levels for the rest of the day.

You can go for a walk or run, hit the gym, throw on a P90X or Insanity DVD, watch a yoga video on YouTube, or find a Life S.A.V.E.R.S. buddy to play some early morning racquetball. There's also an excellent app called *7 Minute Workout* that gives you a full body workout in—you guessed it—seven minutes. The choice is yours—just pick one and do it.

As a salesperson, you are on the go. You need an endless reserve of energy to capitalize on all of the opportunities that are going to come your way, and a daily morning exercise practice is going to provide it.

Exercise for Your Brain

Even if you don't care about your physical health, consider that exercise is simply going to make you smarter, and that can only help your sales. Dr. Steven Masley, a Florida physician and nutritionist with a health practice geared toward executives, explains how exercise creates a direct connection to your cognitive ability.

"If we're talking about brain performance, the best predictor of brain speed is aerobic capacity—how well you can run up a hill is very strongly correlated with brain speed and cognitive shifting ability," Masley said.

Masley has designed a corporate wellness program based on the work he's done with more than 1,000 patients. "The average person going into these programs will increase brain speed by 25-30 percent."

Imagine how a 25–30 percent increase in brain speed could increase your ability to respond to clients in a positive way and offer helpful solutions. How much could you increase your sales just by having more effective and efficient conversations with prospects? Picture yourself getting on the phone with clients after a workout. What would your state of mind be? How different would you feel? What would your customers gain from these conversations? What might that do for your business?

Hal chose yoga and began practicing it shortly after he created *The Miracle Morning*. He's been doing it and loving it ever since. My exercise routine rotates between yoga, the elliptical, and some free weight exercises. I enjoy the variety. Find what resonates with you, and make it a part of your *Miracle Morning*.

Final Thoughts on Exercise

You know that, if you want to maintain good health and increase your energy, you must exercise consistently. That's not news to anyone. But what also isn't news is how easy it is to make excuses. Two of the biggest are "I don't have time" and "I'm too tired." And those are just the first two on the list. There is no limit to the excuses that you can think of. And the more creative you are, the more excuses you can come up with!

That's the beauty of incorporating exercise into your *Miracle Morning*—it happens before your day wears you out, and before you have an entire day to come up with new excuses! Because it happens first, *The Miracle Morning* is really a surefire way to avoid all of those excuses, and to make exercise a daily habit.

Legal disclaimer: Hopefully this goes without saying, but you should consult your doctor or physician before beginning any exercise regimen, especially if you are experiencing any physical pain, discomfort, disabilities, etc. You may need to modify or even refrain from your exercise routine to meet your individual needs.

R is for Reading

One of the fastest ways to achieve everything you want is to model successful people. For every goal you have, there's a good chance there's an expert out there who has already achieved the same thing, or something similar. As Tony Robbins says, success leaves clues.

Fortunately, some of the best of the best have shared their stories throughout history in the form of writing. And that means all those success blueprints are just waiting out there for anyone willing to invest some time in reading. Books are a limitless supply of help and mentorship, right at your fingertips.

If you're thinking, *Uh, yeah, I don't read "self-help" books*, you do not know what you're missing out on! Books are a wealth of knowledge, boundless growth, life changing ideas, and information from some of the most brilliant, successful individuals in the world. Who in their right mind would choose not to take advantage of that?

Want to be a multi-millionaire salesperson? Looking to build better relationships with clients? Do you want to generate more referral business? Hoping to take your sales skills to a level ten?

There are plenty of books, in addition to this one, written by those who have achieved super sales success. Here are some of our favorites:

On Selling:

- *High Trust Selling* by Todd Duncan
- *Influence* by Robert B. Cialdini
- *The Sales Bible* by Jeffrey Gitomer
- *The 10X Rule* by Grant Cardone
- *7L: The Seven Levels of Communication* by Michael J. Maher
- *The Greatest Salesman in the World* by Og Mandino
- *The SPEED of Trust* by Stephen M.R. Covey
- *Go for No!* by Richard Fenton and Andrea Waltz

On Mindset:

- *The One Thing* by Gary Keller and Jay Papasan
- *The Game of Life and How to Play It* by Florence Scovel Shinn
- *The Compound Effect* by Darren Hardy
- *Taking Life Head On* by Hal Elrod
- *Think and Grow Rich* by Napoleon Hill

In addition to finding sales success, you can transform your relationships, increase your self-confidence, improve your communication or persuasion skills, learn how to become healthy, and improve any other area of your life you can think of. Head to your local bookstore—or do what I do and head to Amazon.com—and you'll find more books than you can possibly imagine on any area of your life you want to improve.

For a complete list of our favorite personal development books—including those that have made the biggest impact on our success and happiness—check out the Recommended Reading list at TMMBook.com.

How Much Should You Read?

I recommend making a commitment to read a minimum of 10 pages per day (although five is okay to start with if you read slowly or don't yet enjoy reading).

I know 10 pages doesn't seem like much. But let's do the math. Reading 10 pages a day gives you 3,650 pages a year. That stacks up to approximately eighteen 200-page personal development/self-improvement books! And all in 10-15 minutes of reading, or 15-30 minutes if you read more slowly.

Let me ask you, if you read 18 personal development or sales books in the next year, do you think you'll be more knowledgeable, capable, and confident? Do you think you'll be a better you? Absolutely! Reading 10 pages read per day is not going to break you, but it will sure make you.

Final Thoughts on Reading

- Begin with the end in mind—what do you hope to gain from a book? Take a moment to do this now by asking yourself what you want to gain from reading this one.

- Many *Miracle Morning* practitioners use their Reading time to catch up on their religious texts, such as the Bible or Torah.

- Don't be afraid to underline, circle, highlight, dog-ear, and take notes in the margins of this book. The process of marking books as you read allows you to come back at any time and recapture all of the key lessons, ideas, and benefits without needing to read the book again, cover to cover. If you read on a digital reader, such as Kindle, Nook, or via iBooks, notes and highlighting are easily organized, so you can see them each time you flip through the book, or you can go directly to a list of your notes and highlights.

- Summarize key ideas, insights and memorable passages in your journal. You can build your own brief summary of your favorite books so you can revisit the key content anytime in just minutes.

- Rereading good personal development books is an underutilized yet very effective strategy. Rarely can you read a book once and internalize all of the value from that book. Achieving mastery in any area requires repetition. I've read books like *Think and Grow Rich* as many as three times and often refer back to them throughout the year. Why not try it out with this book? Commit to rereading it as soon as you're finished, to deepen your learning and give yourself more time to master *The Miracle Morning*.

- Take advantage of action steps and action plans set out in the books you read. While reading is a great way to learn new strategies, it is the implantation and practice of these new strategies that will really improve your life and business. Are committed to implementing what you're learning by taking action and following through with at least one of the 30-Day Challenges at the end of each chapter?

S is for Scribing

Scribing is simply another word for writing (thanks thesaurus, I owe you one). I write in my journal for five to ten minutes during my *Miracle Morning*, usually during reading time, and then during an additional period of contemplation. By getting your thoughts out of your head and putting them in writing, you gain valuable insights you'd otherwise never see.

The Scribing element of your *Miracle Morning* enables you to document your insights, ideas, breakthroughs, realizations, successes, and lessons learned, as well as any areas of opportunity, personal growth, or improvement. Use your journal to note your sales strengths, what went right in each day's sales calls and meetings, and add any distinctions you want to remember later and perhaps work on.

If you're like Hal, you probably have at least a few half-used and barely touched journals and notebooks. It wasn't until he started his own *Miracle Morning* practice that it quickly became a favored habit. As Anthony Robbins said, "A life worth living is a life worth recording."

Writing will give you the daily benefits of consciously directing your thoughts, but what's even more powerful are insights you'll gain from reviewing your journals, from cover to cover, afterwards—especially, at the end of the year.

It is hard to put into words how overwhelmingly constructive the experience of going back and reviewing your journals can be. *The Miracle Morning for Real Estate Agents* co-author Michael Maher is, naturally, an avid practitioner of the Life S.A.V.E.R.S. Part of Michael's morning routine is to write down his appreciations and affirmations in what he calls his Blessings Book. Michael says it best:

"What you appreciate…APPRECIATES. It is time to take our insatiable appetite for what I want and replace it with an insatiable appetite for what I do have. Write your appreciations, be grateful and appreciative, and you will have more of those things you crave—better relationships, more material goods, more happiness."

There is strength in writing down what you appreciate, and reviewing this material can change your mindset on a challenging day.

While there are many worthwhile benefits of keeping a daily journal, here are a few more of my favorites. With daily scribing, you'll:

- Gain Clarity—Journaling will give you more clarity and understanding and allow you to brainstorm, as well as help you work through problems.

- Capture Ideas—You will capture and be able to expand on your ideas, and journaling also prevents you from losing the important ones you are saving for an opportune moment in the future.

- Review Lessons—Journaling provides a place to reference and review all of the lessons you've learned.

- Acknowledge Your Progress—It's wonderful to go back and re-read your journal entries from a year ago and see how much progress you've made. It's one of the most empowering, confidence-inspiring, and enjoyable experiences. It can't really be duplicated any other way.

Effective Journaling

Here are three simple steps to get started with journaling or improve your current journaling process.

1. Choose a Format: Physical or Digital. You'll want to decide up front if you want to go with a traditional, physical lined journal, or go with a digital journal (such as on your computer or an app for your phone or tablet). The easiest way to decide is to ask yourself if you prefer to write by hand or type.

2. Get a Journal. Almost anything can work, but when it comes to a physical journal, there is something to be said for getting a nice, durable journal that you enjoy looking at—after all, ideally you're going to have it for the rest of your life. I recommend getting a journal that is not only lined, but also dated, with room to write for all 365 days of the year. I've found that having a pre-designated (dated) space to write keeps you accountable to follow through each day, since you can't help but notice when you miss a day or two.

Here are a few of my favorite physical journals:

- *Five Minute Journal* (FiveMinuteJournal.com) has become very popular among top performers. It has a very specific format for each day, giving you prompts, such as "I am grateful for..." and "What would make today great?" It literally takes five minutes or less, and includes an "Evening" option, which allows you to review your day.

- *The Miracle Morning Journal* (available on Amazon or at MiracleMorningJournal.com) is designed specifically to enhance and support your Miracle Morning, and to keep you organized and accountable to keep track of your Life S.A.V.E.R.S. each day. You can also download a free sample of *The Miracle Morning Journal* today at TMMbook.com to make sure it's right for you.

- BulletJournal.com. It's not actually a journal you buy, it's a journal system you incorporate into the journal of your choosing.

If you prefer to use a digital journal, there are also many choices available. Here are a few of my favorites:

- Five Minute Journal (FiveMinuteJournal.com) also offers an iPhone app, which follows the same format as the physical version but also sends you helpful reminders to input your entries each morning and evening. It also allows you to upload photos to create visual memories.

- Day One (DayOneApp.com) is a popular journaling app, and it's perfect if you don't want any structure or any limits on how much you can write. Day One offers a blank page, so if you like to write lengthy journal entries, this may be the app for you.

- Penzu (Penzu.com) is a very popular online journal, which doesn't require an iPhone, iPad, or Android device. All you need is a computer.

Again, it really comes down to your preference and which features you want. Type "online journal" into Google or "journal" into the app store, and you'll get a variety of choices.

Customizing the Life S.A.V.E.R.S.

I want to share a few ideas specifically geared toward customizing the Life S.A.V.E.R.S. based on your schedule and preferences. Your current morning routine might allow you to fit in only a six-, twenty- or thirty-minute *Miracle Morning*, or you might choose to do a longer version on the weekends.

Here is an example of a fairly common, 60-minute *Miracle Morning* schedule, using the Life S.A.V.E.R.S.

Silence: 10 minutes

Affirmations: 10 minutes

Visualization: 5 minutes

Exercise: 10 minutes

Reading: 20 minutes

Scribing: 5 minutes

You can customize the sequence, too. Some people prefer to do their exercise first, as a way to increase their blood flow and wake themselves up. However, you might prefer to do exercise as your last activity in the Life S.A.V.E.R.S. so you're not sweaty during your *Miracle Morning*. Personally, I prefer to start with a period of peaceful, purposeful silence so that I can wake up slowly, clear my mind, and focus my energy and intentions. I save exercise for last so that way I can jump directly into the shower and proceed with the rest of my day. However, this is your *Miracle Morning*, not mine—feel free to experiment with different sequences and see which you like best.

Final Thoughts on the Life S.A.V.E.R.S.

Everything is difficult before it's easy. Every new experience is uncomfortable before it's comfortable. The more you practice the Life S.A.V.E.R.S. the more natural and normal each of them will feel. Hal's first time meditating was almost his last, as his mind raced like a Ferrari and his thoughts bounced around uncontrollably like the silver sphere in a pinball machine. Now, he loves meditation, and while he's still no master, he says he's decent at it.

Similarly, my first time doing yoga I felt like a fish out of water. I wasn't flexible, couldn't do the poses correctly, and felt awkward and uncomfortable. Now, yoga is one of my favorite forms of exercise, and I'm so glad that I stuck with it.

I invite you to begin practicing the Life S.A.V.E.R.S. now, so you can become familiar and comfortable with each of them and get a jump-start before you begin The Miracle Morning 30-Day Life Transformation Challenge in chapter 11.

If your biggest concern is still finding time, don't worry; I've got you covered. You can actually do the entire *Miracle Morning*—receiving the full benefits from all six of the Life S.A.V.E.R.S.—in only six minutes a day! Just do each of the Life S.A.V.E.R.S. for one minute each: close your eyes and enjoy a moment of silence, visualize your goals as achieved, say your affirmations (or repeat your favorite affirmation over and over). You can then do jumping jacks or push-ups or crunches, then grab a book and read a paragraph, and then jot down a few thoughts in your journal. These six minutes will serve to set you on the right path for the day—and you can always devote more time later in the day when your schedule permits or the opportunity presents itself.

TOP ONE PERCENT SALESPERSON INTERVIEW
Mariana Pryhuber – Sales Consultant, Paperly

Mariana has become a top producer in only a couple short years at Paperly, offering customized paper products including cards and personalized stationery. Though her direct sales career has been short, with her experience in purchasing for large retail stores and her desire to constantly improve, there is little question how she found her way to the top one percent even while working only part-time.

Mariana recognizes the importance of personal growth, and she understands the need for maintaining a positive mental attitude. "To help start and end the day in a positive way, I have several affirmations written out on my mirror. I see them every morning and every night and repeat them. I also like to take a minute each day and focus on all that I have to be grateful for."

While Marianna does not lack confidence, she arms herself against fear and failure with powerful affirmations to start each day. She uses them to set expectations for the day, to remember what she is grateful for, and to start the day with power and purpose.

MIRACLE MORNING SUCCESS STORY
Dr. Todd Boggs – Owner, Chiropractic
Concepts

Before I read *The Miracle Morning*, I considered myself successful on many levels, but felt as though I could be so much more. It seemed like I would keep spinning my wheels and not get as much accomplished as I wanted.

Just wanted to say thank you for your book and what it has helped me accomplish in the first three months I have implemented it. I have made $30,000 more in the last two months, compared to last year, and the only difference is using the *Life S.A.V.E.R.S.* each day. I am more focused and disciplined and enjoy reading like never before and working on myself to be the best that I can be.

My wife and I even bought 30 copies of *The Miracle Morning* to give to the high school graduates that we have received announcements for this year.

I look forward to many great *Miracle Mornings* to come! I feel like the sky is the limit, and I am excited to get out of bed and start the day early. I always knew that *The Miracle Morning* steps were important but did not know how exactly to implement them until I read *The Miracle Morning*. I cannot wait to see what the future holds for me and my newfound productivity.

— 4 —
SELF-LEADERSHIP

> *"Mastering others is strength. Mastering yourself is true power."*
> —LAO TZU

You're a salesperson, so you know how hard (read: impossible) it is to sell others on something if you aren't sold on it yourself.

Salespeople, after all, are problem solvers. Your job is to help people solve their problems by presenting them with effective, and often customized, solutions. If you don't believe a product or service is up to the job, it's impossible to sell it.

What you may not realize, though, is that as a salesperson you are also a leader. You're leading your prospective customer to make the best buying decision by guiding them through your selling process. And just as it's impossible to sell something if you don't believe in it yourself, it's impossible to lead others if you don't know how to effectively lead yourself.

To find the happiness and success you desire and deserve, you must master the key principles of self-leadership. To grow your sales, in other words, you need to grow yourself.

As summed up by Andrew Bryant, founder of Self-Leadership International, "*Self-leadership is the practice of intentionally influencing your thinking, feelings, and behaviors to achieve your objective(s). It is having a developed sense of who you are, what you can do, and where you are going combined with the ability to influence your communication, emotions, and behaviors on the way to getting there.*"

Before I reveal the key principles of self-leadership, I want to share with you what I've discovered about the crucial role that mindset plays as the foundation of effective self-leadership. Your past beliefs, self-image, and the ability to collaborate with and rely upon others at integral times will factor into your ability to excel as a self-leader.

Be Aware and Skeptical of Your Self-Imposed Limitations

You may be holding onto false limiting beliefs that are subconsciously interfering with your ability to achieve your sales goals.

For example, you may be someone who repeats, "I wish I was more motivated" or "I wish I were better at getting appointments," yet in reality you are more than capable of generating motivation and filling your calendar with sales appointments. Thinking of yourself as less than capable is assuming imminent failure, and thwarting your ability to succeed.

Effective self-leaders closely examine their beliefs, decide which ones serve them, and eliminate the ones that don't.

When you find yourself stating anything that sounds like a limiting belief, from "I don't have enough time," to "I could never do that," pause and turn your self-limiting statements into empowering questions, such as: *Where can I find more time in my schedule? How could I do that?*

Doing this allows you to tap into your inborn creativity and find a way to make anything happen. There's always a way, when you're committed.

See Yourself as Better than You've Ever Been

As Hal wrote in *The Miracle Morning*, most of us suffer from Rearview Mirror Syndrome, limiting our current and future results based on who we were in the past. You must remember, although *where you are is a result of who you were, where you go depends entirely on who you choose to be from this moment forward.*

All successful salespeople—especially the top one percent in any company or industry—at one point made the choice to see themselves as better than they had ever been before. They stopped maintaining limiting beliefs based on their *past*, and instead started forming their beliefs based on their unlimited *potential*.

One of the best ways to do this is to follow the four-step formula for creating affirmations that was outlined in chapter 3. Be sure to create affirmations that reinforce what's possible for you and remind you of whom you're committed to becoming.

Actively Seek Support

I've coached hundreds of people through the processes of identifying their areas of strength and weaknesses, coming to grips with their innate talents and abilities, and engaging the support they need. I've found that those that struggle the most are those that suffer in silence: they assume everyone else has greater capabilities, and they all but refuse to seek help and assistance.

If that describes you, then this might help: every single person that we interviewed for this book was not only a true top one percent achiever, but each has a team that supports them. They know what they excel at, and they know where they fall short. Not only have they eventually embraced the gaps and found solutions, they are just fine with their humanity.

Self-leaders know that they need a team to provide the support they need to get things done. You might need administrative support, for example, so you can do what you do best: close sales! You may need accountability support to overcome your tendency to procrastinate. We all need support in different areas of our lives, and a great self-leader understands that and uses it to her benefit.

The Five Core Principles of Self-Leadership

To grow, and become a top seller, you'll need to become a top self-leader. My favorite way to cut the learning curve in half and decrease the time it takes for you to reach the top one percent is to model the traits and behaviors of those who have reached the top before you.

During my fifteen years in sales, I've seen many leaders and a myriad of effective strategies. Here are the five I believe will shave years off of your pursuit of self-leadership excellence:

1. Take 100 Percent Responsibility

2. Become Financially Free

3. Put Fitness First

4. Systematize Your World

5. Commit to Your Process

Principle #1: Take 100 Percent Responsibility

Here's the hard truth: If you're not achieving the life you want right now, it's all on you.

The sooner you take ownership of that fact, the sooner you'll begin to move forward. This isn't meant to be harsh—the most successful salespeople in the world are rarely victims. In fact, one of the reasons they are successful is that they take absolute, total, and complete responsibility for each and every single thing in their lives, whether it's personal or professional, good or bad, their job or someone else's.

While average people waste their time blaming and complaining, achievers are busy creating the results and circumstances they want for their lives. While mediocre salespeople are complaining to their manager that none of their prospects have any money, successful salespeople have taken responsibility for finding the prospects that do. And, they're turning those prospects into customers.

My paradigm shifted when I heard Hal giving the keynote speech at our national sales conference, and he said the following:

"The moment you take 100 percent responsibility for *everything* in your life is the same moment you claim the power to change *anything* in your life. But you must understand that responsibility is not the same thing as blame. Blame determines who is at fault for something; responsibility determines who is committed to improving a situation. It rarely matters who is at fault; what matters is that YOU are committed to improving your situation."

When you take true ownership of your life, there's no time for discussing whose fault something is, or who gets the blame. Playing the blame game is easy, but there's no longer any place for it in your life. Finding reasons for why you didn't make your quota or close those sales is for the other guy, not you! You own your results; you make them happen. You always have a choice about how you respond or react in any and every situation.

Here's the psychological shift I suggest you make: take ownership and stewardship over all of your decisions, actions, and outcomes, starting right now. Replace unnecessary blame with total responsibility. From now on, there's no doubt as to who is at the wheel, and who is responsible for all of your results. You make the calls, do the follow up, decide the outcomes you want and you get them. Your results are 100 percent your responsibility. Right? The reality is that you can't change what's in the past, but the good news is that you can change everything else.

Remember: you are in the position of power, you are in control, and there are no limits to what you can accomplish.

Principle #2: Become Financially Free

How is your financial situation? Are you earning significantly more money each month than you need to survive? Are you able to save, invest, and share part of your income on a regular basis? Are you debt-free with a large reserve that allows you to capitalize on opportunities that come your way and ride out unexpected challenges? If so, congratulations: you're among a very small percentage of people who live their lives from a place of abundance.

If not, don't be too hard on yourself; you're not alone. The majority of people have less than $10,000 to their name, and an average of $16,000 in unsecured debt. No judgment here if this describes you, I'm simply going to point you right back to Principle #1 and encourage you to take 100 percent responsibility for your financial situation.

I've seen and heard every reason for someone to dive deep into debt, fail to save, and not have a nest egg. None of those matter now. Yes, the best time to have started saving a percentage of your income was five, ten, or even twenty years ago. But the next best time is right now. Whether you're twenty, or forty, or sixty years old, it's never too late to take control of your personal finances. You'll find an incredible boost in energy from taking charge, and you'll be able to use your accumulated savings to create even more wealth because you'll actually have money to invest in new opportunities. Sounds good, right?

Financial freedom isn't something you achieve overnight. It is a result of developing the mindset and the habits *now* that will take you down the path that leads to financial freedom.

Here are the three steps you can do right now to get you started on your path:

1. Set aside 10 percent of your income to save and invest. In fact, I recommend your start with taking 10 percent of whatever you have in the bank right now and put it in a savings account. (Go ahead, I'll wait.) Make whatever adjustments you need to make to your lifestyle to be able to live off of 90 percent of your current income.

2. Take another 10 percent and give it away. Most wealthy people give a percentage of their income to causes they believe in. But you don't have to wait until you're wealthy to start this practice. Tony Robbins said, "If you won't give $1 out of $10, you'll never give $1 million out of $10 million." Can't do 10 percent or the rent check will bounce? Fine, start with 5, 2, or 1 percent. It's not the amount that matters, but developing the mindset and creating the habit that will change your financial future and serve you for the rest of your life. You've got to start teaching your subconscious brain that you are abundant—that there's more than enough, and there is always more on the way.

3. Continuously educate yourself on the topic of money.
It's one of the most important topics for you to master, and you can start by adding the following books to your reading list (which cover various aspects of financial freedom):

- *Secrets of the Millionaire Mind* by T. Harv Eker
- *MONEY: Master the Game* by Tony Robbins
- *The Total Money Makeover* by Dave Ramsey
- *The Millionaire Fastlane* by MJ DeMarco
- *Rich Dad Poor Dad* by Robert Kiyosaki

Principle #3: Put Fitness First

How's your health these days? Can you wake up before your alarm and do what's important, handle all the demands of the day, and put out the inevitable fires, all without ending the day exhausted and out of breath?

I discussed exercise as part of the Life S.A.V.E.R.S., and yes, I'm going to discuss it again right now. It's a fact that the state of your health and fitness is a huge factor in your energy and success levels—especially for salespeople. Doing what's required to keep deals coming in requires a ton of energy and sales is an energy sport. Like any sport, you need an almost endless supply of energy and stamina.

To do all those presentations, be constantly prospecting for new customers, and ensuring each and every client is satisfied can be exhausting. If you are overweight, out of shape, and constantly out of breath, setting bigger and bigger sales goals is, in our opinion, a recipe for disaster. You will feel not only like there's more month than money, you may also feel like there's more day than energy.

The great news is that this is completely within your control!

Here are three practices of top performers that you can use to ensure that your health, fitness, and energy levels fully support your sales goals and objectives:

1. **Eat and drink to win.** Put very simply, everything you ingest either contributes to your health or detracts from it. Drinking water puts a check in the plus column; double shots of tequila probably won't. Eating fresh fruits and vegetables equals more plusses. Rolling through the drive-through to wolf down some fast food, not so much. I know you know the drill. This isn't rocket science, but you do need to stop fooling yourself. Become aware of what you're eating and how it's affecting your performance on the sales field. We'll dive deeper into this in the next chapter: Energy Engineering.

2. **Sleep to win.** Getting enough rest is as critical to sales performance as what you do or don't have in your diet. A good night's sleep provides the basis for a day of peak performance, clear thought, and sale after successful sale. You probably already know how many hours you need to be at your best. Reverse engineer your schedule so you are asleep in plenty of time to get all of the rest you need to perform at your best.

3. **Exercise to win.** It is no coincidence that you rarely see top performers who are terribly out of shape. Most invest 30–60 minutes of their time each day to hit the gym or the running trail because they understand the importance that daily exercise plays in their success. And while the "E" in S.A.V.E.R.S. ensures that you're going to start each day with 5–10 minutes of exercise, we recommended that you engage in 30–60 minute workouts at least 3–5 times per week. Doing so will ensure that your fitness level supports the energy and confidence you need to succeed.

Principle #4: Systematize Your World

I'm going to discuss in chapters 7, 8, and 9 the sales strategies and systems I believe will be the most helpful to you, but effective self-leaders have systems for just about everything from work activities like scheduling, follow up, entering orders, and sending thank you cards, to personal activities such as sleeping, eating, dealing with money, cars, and family responsibilities. Those systems make life easier, and ensure they are always ready to perform.

Here are three examples of basic systems (the third one being the ultimate game changer):

1. **Daily Attire**—In addition to being a team leader and business coach, I run a real estate sales team in another office, have three children, and I have spent the last two and half years completing this book. As you can imagine, there is not a moment of time to spare. In order to ensure that I do not have to waste any time preparing in the morning, and to make sure I have proper professional attire, my set of dress shirts is dropped every two weeks at the dry cleaners and picked up two days later cleaned and pressed. With fifteen dress shirts, I can get through the whole month in two trips to the cleaners. It sounds simple, but that extra fifteen minutes every morning adds up in the course of a week.

2. **Travel**—Hal, in addition to being a bestselling author, is a speaker who is on the road week after week, sharing *The Miracle Morning* message with audiences around the country and abroad. Collecting the items he needed for every trip was time-consuming, inefficient, and ineffective as he would often forget something back at home or his office. After the third time he forgot the charger for his computer and had to find an Apple store to buy a $99 replacement (ouch) or ask the front desk for a phone charger, shaver, or an extra set of cufflinks left behind by a previous guest, he'd had enough. He assembled a travel bag containing every single item he needs for his trips, and now he can leave at a moment's notice because his bag contains everything he needs to conduct business on the road—business cards, brochures, copies of his books, adaptors and chargers for his phone and computer, even earplugs in case his hotel room neighbor is a noisy guest.

You'll know you need a system when you have a challenge that is recurring or you find you're missing opportunities because you're unprepared. If you're walking out the door with just enough time to make an appointment only to discover you're running on fumes, you need a system for getting out the door earlier: pack your briefcase the night before, have your clothes already cleaned and pressed, set the coffee maker, get up earlier, etc. Said another way, wherever you feel like you need to get your act together, you need a system. A life without systems is a life with unnecessary stress!

3. **Time-Blocking**—I am going to share something with you that will totally change your ability to produce consistent sales results. Many of you may even want to slap yourselves when you hear the easiest way to own results because it is something that almost all salespeople have been taught and almost none of them do effectively on a consistent basis: *You must have a pre-determined action plan filled with the activities that will get you to your goal, put all the activities into a time-blocked daily schedule, and live by it.* If you write it in your schedule, you must do it. That is owning your results at a high level.

That's not to say you cannot have any flexibility in your schedule. In fact we strongly suggest you plan plenty of family and recreation time in your calendar. You can move things on occasion as needed, but you must do all of the activities in your calendar. When you do this, achieving your goals is no longer a matter of if, but only a matter of when.

One of the main reasons that this technique is so effective is because it takes the emotional roller coaster caused by results out of the decision making for your daily activities. How many times has an appointment gone bad and then it ruined your day? Chances are, nothing else was accomplished. If you followed your calendar though, and the calendar said networking event, writing ads, or making calls, and you were committed to the calendar, then you have a fruitful afternoon. Take control. Stop letting outside influences manage your calendar. Start blocking your time, and follow through, no matter what.

If you find you need additional support around this, do what several of my coaching clients do: send a copy of your calendar to a coach, a manager, and accountability partner and have them hold you accountable. Your commitment to this one skill will allow you to take full responsibility for your level of activity in order to create results.

There's no need to reinvent the wheel to create a system—someone has struggled with, and overcome, any challenge you are faced with. If ideas escape you, find the closest person who excels at what you struggle with and ask their advice! Chances are, they are on the same path as you, just a little further ahead. Soon, you'll have the systems you need and the extra energy they provide.

Principle #5: Commit to Your Process

If there is any not-so-obvious secret to sales success, this is it: **Commit to your process (without being emotionally attached to your results).** Every result that you desire—from improving your physique to increasing your sales—is preceded by a process that is required to produce the result. When you define YOUR process, and commit to it for an extended period of time, the results take care of themselves. There's no need to ever stress or worry about how a day, week, or even a month of selling goes—so long as you're committed to your process over the long haul.

Yet, as human beings, it is natural for us to be emotionally attached to our short-term results. It's human nature. As salespeople, we let a bad day on the phone cause us to feel bad. We allow a discouraging day of appointments to discourage us. When our sales are down, we feel down. We ride the emotional roller coaster of being a salesperson, and our emotional attachment to our results negatively affects our commitment to our process. But does it have to be that way? It absolutely does not.

Hal had this realization at just 21 years old, which he credits much of his selling success to. "I realized that if I committed to making X number of calls each day (my process), the law of averages would all but ensure that I could count on X number of sales each month, quarter, and year. So, it only made sense to commit to my process—a predetermined number of daily calls—and there was no reason to worry or to get so stressed out over my day-to-day results. Then I realized that if I simply increased my number of daily calls by any percentage, I would, by default, increase my sales (and my income) by the same percentage. Double my calls, and I would double my sales. It almost seemed too simple, but it worked like clockwork."

Salespeople who produce consistent results, that top one percent who are the very best at putting impressive sales numbers on the board, simply take consistent action. To become a top one per-cent-er, you can't take some action. You can't take a little action. You can't do it only when you feel like it or only when you're inspired. You have to define your daily *process* and take consistent action, day in and day out, for an extended period of time. The good news is that someday you will be on such a roll you will have so much momentum you may not need to work as hard or as smart. As your skill and your numbers improve, your process can be tweaked and upgraded, to achieve greater results.

But until that day comes, until you have a major capital re-serve, have eliminated all debt, and gotten yourself to where you really want to be, you've got to put in the time and effort. There are no exceptions and no substitutions for committing to your process (without being emotionally attached to your results).

In the chapters that follow I'll give you the insight and direc-tion you need to take consistent action. For now, you'll need to prepare your mind to keep going even when the results you want aren't coming fast enough, and to have the stamina to withstand plenty of rejection and disappointment. The top one percent aren't the very best because they make a few calls on a semi-regular basis. They are consistent, persistent, and unfailing in their dedication to taking action every single day, and you need to be the same!

Where is Your Self-Control?

Self-control is the ability to control impulses and reactions, and is another name for self-discipline.

Before you skip this section because you think self-control is some kind of negative and limiting behavior, let me assure you it's quite the opposite! When used wisely and with common sense, self-control becomes one of the most important tools for self-im-provement and sales success.

Self-control is vital for overcoming not just the fear you might have around the sales process, it is also helpful when addressing addictions or any kind of incongruous behavior. Self-control puts you in control of your life and your behavior in life, and in sales. It improves your relationships, develops patience and tolerance, and is an important tool for attaining success and happiness. Imagine having the self-control to handle anything that comes your way?

How does self-control help you? Let me count the ways...

- Keeps in check self-destructive, addictive, obsessive, and compulsive behavior.
- Gives you a sense of mastery and balance in your life.
- Helps to keep inappropriate emotional responses in check.
- Eliminates feelings of helplessness and dependency on others.
- Helps to manifest mental and emotional detachment (really important in sales!), which contributes to peace of mind.
- Enables you to control your moods and reject negative feelings and thoughts.
- Strengthens self-esteem, confidence, inner strength, self-mastery, and willpower.
- Enables you to take charge of your life.
- Makes you a responsible and trustworthy human being.

What prevents self-control?

- Lack of knowledge and understanding of what self-control really is.
- Strong and uncontrolled emotional responses.
- Reacting to outside stimuli without thinking.
- Lack of discipline and willpower.
- Lack of the desire to change and improve.
- Seeing self-control as a limiting and unpleasant activity.
- The belief that self-control eliminates fun.
- Lack of faith in yourself and in your abilities.

How to Develop Self-Control

1. First, you need to identify the areas of your life in which you need to gain more self-control. Where do you find yourself lacking in self-control?

   Possible areas could be:

   - Eating
   - Spending
   - Drinking
   - Working
   - Gambling
   - Smoking
   - Obsessive behavior

2. Try to identify the emotions that indicate a lack of control, such as anger, dissatisfaction, unhappiness, resentment, pleasure, or fear.

3. Identify the thoughts and beliefs that push you to behave in an uncontrolled manner.

4. Several times a day, especially when you need to display self-control, repeat one of the following affirmations for one to two minutes:

   - I am fully in control of myself.
   - I have the power to choose my emotions and thoughts.
   - Self-control brings me inner strength and leads me to success.
   - I am in control of my reactions.
   - I am in charge of my behavior.
   - I am gaining control of my emotions.
   - I am the master of my life.
   - Day by day, my ability to control my feelings and thoughts is increasing.
   - Self-control is fun and pleasurable.

5. Use the "V" in your Life S.A.V.E.R.S. to visualize yourself act-ing with self-control and self-restraint. Think of an instance where you usually act with a lack of control, and visualize that you are acting calmly and with self-mastery.

Self-Confidence, Self-Esteem, and Attitude

Talk of self-leadership and self-control wouldn't be complete without mention of their close siblings: self-confidence, self-es-teem, and a positive attitude.

Self-confidence is the belief in your ability, skills, and personal power. You have to have self-confidence in order for others to have confidence in you. Experience has taught me that when I am con-fident in what I'm doing, others will naturally follow my lead. As I have become more skilled and my confidence has risen, my sales numbers have increased, doubled, increased, and doubled again. The people I have encountered haven't changed, and what I'm sell-ing has remained basically the same. What has happened is that I have become more open and receptive to what I'm selling, and, as I have gained more and more confidence, my sales have increased right along with it. A coincidence? No way.

Self-esteem is having a realistic respect for yourself. Healthy or positive self-esteem can help you hold your head high, and feel proud of yourself and your actions even when things aren't going well. Self-esteem gives you the courage to try new things and the power to believe in yourself. My success has been directly influ-enced by my self-esteem and I know having it can mean success and a lack of it can mean failure. If you're not making the sales you want to make, lack of self-esteem might be the cause. As Maxwell Maltz, author of *Psycho-Cybernetics*, said, "Low self-esteem is like driving through life with your hand-brake on."

As you read this book, and I suggest you read it more than twice, systematically address areas you know need improvement and expansion. If you know your self-confidence and self-esteem levels could use some boosting, then boost them. Design affirma-tions to increase and develop them over time. Visualize yourself acting with more confidence and raising your personal standards and loving yourself more. Your confidence and self-esteem will rise to match your vision.

An unstoppable positive attitude is the salesperson's greatest tool. You probably already know that with a negative attitude you are going nowhere—and fast! There's no question that salespeople encounter more avoidance and rejection than the average person. In fact, if you're doing sales right, you're being rejected all the time!

Without the right attitude, all that rejection can take a toll. You'll face constant "no's." People won't answer your calls. They may cross the street when they see you coming because they aren't ready to buy. They may not want to buy at all and simply won't tell you. To face that every day requires a bulletproof attitude.

A positive attitude has two important components: positive expectation and a waterproof surface.

First, you have to expect the best. You have to know every morning that today is the day you're going to close the deal. Positive expectation is based on conviction and you need to be overflowing with conviction about what you expect to happen today, this week, next week, and on and on. You have to just know you're going to get a call out of the blue by someone who's ready to buy. You need to be positive the guy you've followed up with 74 times is going to be a *yes* the next time you call.

But what happens when it doesn't? Well, if you've ever seen water roll off a duck's back, you've seen waterproofing in action. The duck's back (the feathers) is coated in oil, and water and oil don't mix. Your attitude needs to be like the duck's back in that when you get rejected, avoided, hung up on, or anything else that isn't a *yes*, it rolls right off of you.

By now I hope you've gained a sense of how critical your personal development is in creating a successful sales career. Next, we're going to tackle how to create more than enough energy to be as successful as you want to be!

Your Sales Accelerator Steps

Remember, taking your sales to the next level starts with taking yourself to the next level. Developing self-leadership puts you in control of your life. It eliminates the victim mentality, and ensures you make measurable and swift progress toward sales success.

Step One: Review and integrate the Five Core Principles of Self-Leadership:

1. **Take 100 Percent Responsibility.** Remember, the moment you accept responsibility for *everything* in your life is the moment you claim the power to change *anything* in your life. Your success is 100 percent up to you.

2. **Become Financially Free.** Begin to develop the mindset and habits that will inevitably lead you to a life of financial freedom, including saving a minimum of 10 percent of your income and continuously educating yourself on the topic of money.

3. **Put Fitness First.** If daily fitness isn't already a priority in your life, make it so. In addition to your morning exercise, block time for longer, 30–60 minute workouts 3–5 times each week.

4. **Systematize Your World.** Start putting systems and time-blocked schedules in place so that every day you wake up your result-producing processes have already been predetermined and your success virtually guaranteed. It's then simply a matter of waking up and following through with what you've planned to do when you planned to do it.

5. **Commit to Your Process.** Remember Hal's not-so-obvious secret to sales success: *Commit to your process without being emotionally attached to your results.* Determine which activities you are 100 percent in control of (i.e., prospecting calls) that ultimately produce your results. This is YOUR process. Make your success inevitable by staying committed to your process each day, and let go of any emotional attachment to your short term results since it's your commitment to your daily process that will determine your sales total at the end of the month, quarter, and year.

Step Two: Develop your self-control and upgrade your self-image by using affirmations and visualization. Be sure to customize both at your earliest opportunity—it takes time to see results and the sooner you start, the sooner you'll notice improvements.

TOP ONE PERCENT SALESPERSON INTERVIEW

Josh Mueller – National Champion Sales
Professional, Cutco Cutlery

With over 7,000 clients, a two-time National Champion in his company, and the first to sell over a half million dollars in one year (to residential customers), Josh's highlight reel is littered with success stories. As one of our top one percent performers, Josh offered insights into several of the topics we covered in this chapter on growth.

Josh says, "Stay coachable. Being highly successful is really about leadership (whether you are leading just yourself OR a team). And leadership is a process of self-discovery and improvement. If you're always open to learning and growing then you'll always be moving up. Then, by taking a leadership approach people will naturally want to follow your example."

Josh expands on his beliefs that have taken him to this elite level of success: "I believe in pursuing your work and daily life passionately and fully engaged. I believe that anything is Possible, regardless of your past or current circumstances. I believe in the idea that in order to always be successful you also need to always be growing. I believe that resistance to change is usually the sign that we need to change.

"I believe in delayed gratification. I believe in living below your means and saving more than you spend. I believe that sustainable high performance comes from a healthy body, full of vitality and energy, that is ready and able to perform at the highest level.

"I believe that the choices we make most consistently are a perfect gauge of our current place in life and are great predictors of our trajectory for the future. I believe that within every challenge lies a lesson, and those lessons typically are the most valuable."

MIRACLE MORNING SALESPERSON SUCCESS STORY
George Roberts – Owner, Crucial Networking,
LLC

While already a morning person before discovering *The Miracle Morning*, George's stress and fatigue levels were at an all-time high. "At the time I began reading it, I had been waking at 4:00 a.m. every day for the previous eight weeks to handle work overflow from concurrent projects with tight deadlines, and I was burned out!

Implementing Hal's system has been magical for me. I'm still getting up at 4:00 a.m., but it's MY time. The clarity and accomplishment I feel before 5:00 a.m. changes my day dramatically. I used to start my day like a beach ball, just bouncing around wherever OTHERS dictated I go via their requests. Now I'm like a cannonball, attacking my day with focus.

My stress levels are down, my time with my family is far better spent, and overall I just feel better.

I have lost weight since starting. I stopped fixating on money coming in (or not coming in), and it started flowing automatically. I have a much better relationship with my wife & children. I am no longer punchy and snippy or get very stressed out at circumstances that used to have me teetering on the edge.

I will never miss a *Miracle Morning*! I can't afford to. I love them too much."

— 5 —

Not-So-Obvious Selling Principle #2:

ENERGY ENGINEERING

*"The higher your energy level, the more efficient
your body. The more efficient your body, the better
you feel and the more you will use your talent to
produce outstanding results."*
—ANTHONY ROBBINS

As a salesperson, you live and die by your own steam. You eat what you kill, as they say. Most of the time, if you don't sell, *you don't get paid*.

The trouble, though, isn't that it's all on you. It's that on some days—and I know you've had those days—you wake up and you just don't have the energy or the motivation to hunt. To get out there on those days and face uncertainty, rejection, and disappointment is no easy task. The good days take energy, enthusiasm, and persistence. The hard days? They take all that and more.

Selling requires an abundance of energy. There's no way around it. You can have the best product, the most lucrative territory, the hottest leads, and the most amazing marketing support—but if you don't have the *energy* to take advantage of them, you might as well have no product at all. If you want to sell, you need energy—the more the better, and the more *consistent* the better. After all:

- Energy helps you get out there day after day.
- Energy is contagious—it spreads from you to your clients and prospects like a positive virus, creating symptoms of enthusiasm and *yes* responses everywhere.
- Energy is a vaccine against rejection and disappointment. Get enough of it, and you're almost permanently inoculated against negativity.

The trick then is this: *How do you generate and maintain a high level of sustainable energy, on demand?*

When I'm struggling with energy issues, I can compensate with caffeine and other stimulants, and they'll work for a while... until I crash. You may have noticed the same thing. You can lean on stimulants to build up energy for a short while, but then it seems to fall off just when you need it the most.

If you have been, until now, fueling yourself on coffee and pure determination, you haven't even begun to reach the heights of sales achievement that are possible when you build and tap into the energy you have within you.

Natural Energy Cycles

The first thing to understand about energy is that that the goal isn't to be running at full speed all the time. It isn't practical to maintain a constant full-out energy level. As human beings, there is a natural ebb and flow in our energy levels. Sales, it turns out, is the same. It also goes through intense cycles, such as during the holidays, push periods, major deadlines, and even "quota busters." The trick of energy is to marry, or at least try to sync up, your energy cycles with your sales cycles. You will need to access deeper wells of energy during these particularly intense times throughout your year, and allow yourself the time to rest, rejuvenate and recharge when the intensity lessens.

Just like houseplants need water, our sales energy reserves need regular replenishing. You can go full tilt for long periods of time, but eventually your mind, body, and spirit will need replenishing. Instead of getting to the point of overwhelm, burn out, and maximum stress, why not become proactive about your energy levels, so that they are constantly being replenished, you are consistently rejuvenated, and you have an auto-recharge system in place?

If you have resigned yourself to the fact that you will most likely be tired, cranky, behind on your to do list, out of shape, and unhappy, I have some great news.

Being continually exhausted is not only unacceptable, but *you don't have to settle for it.* There are a few simple ways to get what you need and want—enough rest, time to replenish and recharge, and inner peace and happiness. A tall order? Yes. Impossible? Heck, no!

This is about strategically engineering your life for optimum, sustainable physical, mental, and emotional energy. Here are the three principles I follow to keep my energy reserves at maximum capacity and on tap for whenever I need them.

1. Sleep Smarter

Sleep more, sell more. That might be the most counter-intuitive sales mantra you'll ever hear, but it's true. The body needs enough shut-eye each night to function properly and to recharge after a demanding day. Sleep also plays a critical role in immune function, metabolism, memory, learning, and other vital bodily functions. It's when the body does the majority of its repairing, healing, resting, and growing.

If you don't sleep enough, you're gradually wearing yourself, and your sales, *down.*

Sleeping Versus Sleeping *Enough*

But how much is enough? There is a big difference between the amount of sleep you can get by on and the amount you need to function optimally. Researchers at the University of California, San Francisco discovered that some people have a gene that enables them to do well on six hours of sleep a night. This gene, however, is very rare, appearing in less than 3 percent of the population. For the other 97 percent of us, six hours doesn't come close to cutting it. Just because you're able to function on five to six hours of sleep doesn't mean you wouldn't feel a lot better and actually get more done if you spent an extra hour or two in bed.

That may sound counterintuitive. I can almost hear you thinking: *Spend more time in bed and get more done? How does that work?* But it has been well documented that getting enough sleep allows the body to function at higher levels of performance. That means you'll not only work better and faster, but your attitude will improve, too.

The amount of rest each individual needs every night differs, but research shows that the average adult needs approximately seven to eight hours of sleep to restore the energy it takes to handle all of the demands of living each day.

I have been conditioned, as many of us have, to think I need eight to ten hours of sleep. In fact sometimes I need less, and sometimes I need more. The best way to figure out if you're meeting your sleep needs is to evaluate how you feel as you go about your day. If you're logging enough hours, you'll feel energetic and alert all day long, from the moment you wake up until your regular bedtime. If you're not, you'll reach for caffeine or sugar mid-morning, mid-afternoon … or both.

If you're like most people, when you don't get enough rest, you have difficulty concentrating, thinking clearly, and even remembering things. You might notice your ineffectiveness or inefficiencies at home or at work or even blame these missteps on your busy schedule. The more sleep you miss, the more pronounced your symptoms become.

In addition, a lack of rest and relaxation can really work a number on your mood. Sales is no place for being cranky! It is a scientific fact that when individuals miss out on good nightly rest, their personalities are affected, and they are generally grumpier, less patient, and snap easier. The result of missing out on critical, much-needed rest might make you a bear to be around, which is not much fun for anyone, yourself included.

Most adults cut back on their sleep to pack more activities into their day. Salespeople run against the clock to meet tight deadlines and sales quotas, and they trade sleep for getting more done. Unfortunately, lack of sleep can cause the body to run down, which allows illness, viruses, and diseases the tiny opening they need to attack the body. Because the immune system is not functioning as well as it should, it is susceptible to anything that can compromise it. Eventually, lack of rest can cause sickness and/or missed days or even weeks of work, and that's no way to increase sales.

On the flip side, when you get enough nightly rest, your body runs as it should, you're pleasant to be around, and your immune system is stronger. And that's precisely when you'll make more sales. Think of good sleep as the time when you turn on your inner sales magnet. Wake up rested and in a great mood because of your Life S.A.V.E.R.S., and you'll attract more sales because a happy salesperson is also a rich one.

The True Benefits of Sleep

You may not realize just how powerful sleep actually is. While you're happily wandering through your dreams, sleep is doing some hard work on your behalf, and delivering a host of amazing benefits.

You can improve your memory. Your mind is surprisingly busy while you snooze. During sleep you strengthen memories and practice skills learned while you were awake through a process called consolidation.

"If you are trying to learn something, whether it's physical or mental, you learn it to a certain point with practice," says Dr. David Rapoport, who is an associate professor at NYU Langone Medical Center and a sleep expert, "but something happens while you sleep that makes you learn it better."

In other words, if you're trying to learn something new, whether it's Spanish, a new tennis swing, or the specifications of a new product in your arsenal, you'll perform better when you get adequate sleep.

You can live longer. Too much or too little sleep is associated with a shorter lifespan, although it's not clear if it's a cause or an effect. In a 2010 study of women ages 50–79, more deaths occurred in women who got less than five hours or more than six-and-a-half hours of sleep per night. Getting the right amount of sleep is a good idea for your long-term health.

You can be more creative. Get a good night's sleep before getting out the easel and paintbrushes or the pen and paper. In addition to consolidating memories or making them stronger, your brain appears to reorganize and restructure them, which may result in more creativity as well.

Researchers at Harvard University and Boston College found that people seem to strengthen the emotional components of a memory during sleep, which may help spur the creative process.

You'll attain and maintain a healthy weight more easily. If you're overweight, you won't have the same energy levels as those who are within a healthy weight range. Moreover, if you are changing your lifestyle to include more exercise and diet changes, you'll want to plan an earlier bedtime. Putting additional physical demands on your body means you will need to counter-balance those demands with enough rest.

The good news: researchers at the University of Chicago found that dieters who were well-rested lost more fat—up to 56 percent more—than those who were sleep deprived, who lost more muscle mass. Dieters in the study also felt hungrier when they got less sleep. Sleep and metabolism are controlled by the same sectors of the brain, and when you are sleepy, certain hormones go up in your blood, and those same hormones drive appetite.

You'll feel less stressed. When it comes to our health, stress and sleep are closely connected, and both can affect cardiovascular health. Sleep can definitely reduce stress levels, and with that comes better control of blood pressure. It is also believed that sleep affects cholesterol levels, which play a significant role in heart disease.

You'll avoid mistakes and accidents. The National Highway Traffic Safety Administration reported in 2009 that being tired accounted for the highest number of fatal, single-car, run-off-the-road crashes due to the driver's performance—even more than alcohol! Sleepiness is grossly underrated as a problem by most people, but the cost to society is enormous. Lack of sleep affects reaction time and decision-making.

If insufficient sleep for only one night can be as detrimental to your driving ability as having an alcoholic drink, imagine how it affects your ability to maintain the focus necessary to become a top salesperson.

So, how many hours of sleep do you *really* need? You tell me. Now, if you really struggle with falling or staying asleep, and it is a concern for you, I highly recommend getting a copy of Shawn Stevenson's book, *Sleep Smarter: 21 Proven Tips to Sleep Your Way to a Better Body, Better Health, and Bigger Success*. It's one of the best, most well-researched books that I've seen on the topic of sleep.

2. Rest Your Mind

The conscious counterpart to sleep is *rest*. While some people use the terms interchangeably, they're really quite different. You might get eight hours of sleep, but if all the hours you're awake are spent on-the-go, then you won't have any time to think or recharge your batteries. Working all day and then running from activity to activity after hours, only to end your day with a quick dinner and a late bedtime doesn't allow for any quiet time.

Likewise, spending weekends taking the kids to soccer, volleyball, or basketball, then heading out to see a football game, going to church, singing in the choir, attending several birthday parties, etc. While all of it is great, too much of it doesn't allow for any quiet or rest and recharge time.

We live in a culture that perpetuates the belief that when our lives are busy and exciting, we are more valuable, more important, or more alive. In truth, we are all of those things when we can be at peace within our own skin. Despite our best intentions to live balanced lives, though, the modern world demands that we are almost always connected and productive, and these demands can drain us emotionally, spiritually, and physically.

What if, instead of being constantly on the go, you valued intentional quiet time, sacred space, and silence? How would that change your life, parenting abilities, and your success in sales?

It may seem counterintuitive to take time out when your to-do list is a mile long, but the fact is that doing nothing can make you feel healthier, more energetic, and more alive than not being rested and centered.

Rest melts stress away, and research proves it. Practices like yoga and meditation also lower heart rates, blood pressure, and oxygen consumption and alleviate hypertension, arthritis, insomnia, depression, infertility, cancer, and anxiety. The spiritual benefits of resting are profound. Slowing down and getting quiet means you can actually begin to hear your own wisdom, your inner knowledge, and your inner voice. Rest and its close sibling, relaxation, allow us to reconnect with the world in and around us, inviting ease in our lives and a sense of happy self.

And yes, in case you're wondering, you'll be more productive, nicer to your friends and family members (not to mention your prospects and clients), and in general much happier as well. When we rest, it's like letting the earth lie fallow rather than constantly planting and harvesting. Our personal batteries need to be recharged. The best way is to recharge them is to truly and simply rest.

Easy Ways to Rest

Most of us confuse rest with recreation. To rest, we do things like hike, garden, workout, or even party. Any of these activities can only be termed restful because they are breaks from work, but truthfully they are not, and cannot, be defined as rest.

Instead, rest has been defined as a kind of waking sleep, experienced while you are alert and aware. Rest is the essential bridge to sleep, and we achieve rest and sleep the same way: by making space for them and allowing them to happen. Every living organism needs rest, including you. When we don't take the time to rest, eventually the lack of it takes a toll on the body.

- If you are using five minutes every morning during your Life S.A.V.E.R.S. to meditate or sit in silence, that is a great start.

- You can reserve Sundays or, if Sunday is a busy workday for you, one other day of the week for rest. You can read, watch a movie, do something low-key with family, or even spend time alone. Try cooking at home, playing games with your kids, and enjoying each other's company.

- When you're driving, drive in silence by turning off the radio and stowing your phone.

- Go for a walk without ear buds in your ears. Even a walk in nature without intention or goals, such as burning calories, can work.

- Turn off the television. Designate a half hour, an hour, or even half a day for silence. Try also taking a few conscious breaths, during which you focus on the inhale and exhale or the space between breaths.

- You can also mindfully drink a cup of tea, read something inspirational, write in your journal, take a hot bath, or get a massage.

- Attend a retreat. It could be with your work, a group of friends, your church, any community with which you are involved, family, your spouse, or on your own in nature. On one retreat, we were required to remain silent for an entire evening until morning. It was one of the greatest moments of clarity and peace of my life.

Even taking a nap is a powerful way to rest and recharge. Napping also can lead to better sleep patterns.

It's helpful to set a specific time for rest. You need to put boundaries around it so you can claim that time.

The Rest Habit

Rest certainly isn't something we're taught in school, and you may find you need to learn it and make it a habit—it may not come naturally at first. Practices, such as Yoga Nidra, restorative yoga, and voluntary silence, are powerful ways to go within and achieve restful states of being, particularly when you commit to practicing them regularly.

Learning the benefits of rest through different practices, and bringing them into your everyday life is also an effective way to deeply rest your body, mind, and spirit. Think of how much you and your sales career will benefit from you taking the time to take care of yourself.

3. Eat for Energy

A low energy salesperson sells well below their potential, and when it comes to energy, food may play the most critical role of all. If you're like most people, you make your food choices based on taste first, and consequences second, if at all. Yet, what makes us happy when we eat doesn't always give us maximum energy.

There is nothing wrong with eating foods that taste good, but if you want to be truly healthy and have the energy to sell like a champion, **you must learn to value the energy consequences of the food you eat, above the taste**. Digesting food is one of the most energy-draining processes the body endures (think about how exhausted you feel after a big meal, like Thanksgiving dinner). Thus, **eating living foods that contribute more energy to your body than they require to digest is the secret to maintaining extraordinary levels of energy *all day long***.

Foods like bread, cooked meats, dairy products, and processed foods require a lot of energy to digest and contribute very little energy to your body, leaving you in an energy deficit. Foods like raw fruits, vegetables, nuts, and seeds typically give you more energy than they take, empowering you with an energy surplus to perform at your best.

I have shifted my view of food from that of a reward, treat, or comfort to that of fuel. I want to eat delicious, healthy foods that fuel my energy levels and allow me to keep going as long as I need to go. Technically, food is just fuel for living, *for selling*.

Don't get me wrong, I still enjoy certain foods that are not the healthiest choices, but I strategically reserve them for times when I don't need to maintain optimum energy levels, such as in the evenings and on weekends.

The easiest way for me to start making some better decisions about my eating was to start paying attention to the way I felt after eating certain foods. I literally started setting a timer for 60 minutes, as soon as I finished each meal. One hour later, my timer would go off and I would assess my energy level. It doesn't take much when you are actively recognizing the way your diet affects you. I can clearly tell the difference in my energy level the days that I eat sushi or a salad, and the day I cave for a chicken sandwich or some of that pizza that smells so good. I find that just by incorporating as many of the right foods as I can often stops me from snacking on the unhealthy foods.

The idea is to eat what you need to refuel and recharge your body—to give your body exactly what it needs to generate a sustained energy level. What if you gave your body what it needs to work and play for as long as you like? What if you gave yourself exactly what you truly deserve: the gift of great health, consciously chosen through what you eat and drink?

If you are eating throughout the day almost as an afterthought, maybe hitting a drive-through after you've hit the point of being famished, it could be time to start building a new strategy.

Give some thought to the following:

- Can I start consciously considering the consequences of what I eat (both health and energy consequences), and valuing that above the taste?

- Can I keep water with me at all times so that I can hydrate with intention and purpose and so I can avoid becoming dehydrated?

- Can I plan my meals in advance, including snacks, so I can combat any patterns I have that don't serve me?

Yes, you can do all of these and much more. Think about how much better will your life be, and how many more sales you'll be able to make, when you become conscious and intentional about your eating and drinking habits:

- You will spend more time consciously thinking about food (and truly enjoying the food you eat).
- You will spend less time preparing food.
- You will spend less money on food.
- You will eat less.
- You will get healthier and feel much better.
- Total bonus: You will settle at your natural weight effortlessly.
- Best bonus ever: you'll make more sales, and more money, because you'll look and feel great—you'll be a sales magnet!

Combined with exercise, meditation, and rest, making healthy food choices is a positive step in the right direction for you and your sales career.

As part of your *Miracle Morning,* you have had your first glass of water at the start of the day. I recommend including a full glass of water with each meal, which makes it easier to get in the recommended eight to ten glasses a day. I start and end my days with water. Many mornings, I have already had 48 ounces before I even arrive at work.

I intentionally refuel every three to four hours during the day. My meals consist mostly of some form of protein and vegetables. I snack frequently on fruits, protein bars, chocolate covered raisins, or yogurt. I try to plan my best meals for the days I need to be the most productive.

I believe that eating great most of the time, combined with exercise, gives me the latitude to eat what I want some of the time. I believe I can eat whatever I want, just not always as much as I'd like. I've learned to taste everything, but to eat just enough that I'm satiated.

In the end, here is the simple thing to remember: food is fuel. It serves to get us from the beginning of the day all the way to the end, feeling great and with plenty of energy. Food can be used as the fuel you need, and you can use it to your advantage: to give you the endless energy you need to be the extraordinary salesperson that you are meant to be!

Practice, Practice, Practice

Keep in mind that when you try to adopt these three practices—to sleep, rest, and eat better—you may at first find it uncomfortable. It can be like when you're flying in a jetliner at 30,000 feet: as soon as you start to land, it almost always gets a little bumpy.

Your mind and body experience can be very similar, and you may encounter some "emotional turbulence." Many find it so uncomfortable that they literally flee that turbulence by quickly becoming busy again. Resist the urge to run from the discomfort.

The more you integrate periods of rest and silence into your daily life, the bigger the payoff will be. During more tranquil periods, perhaps you won't need to rest as much, but during periods of intensity (such as meeting a huge quota or a big deadline), more rest and silence than usual might be called for.

As a salesperson, you're in the trenches by default. You'll need to schedule rest, recharging, silence, and self-care in the same way you schedule the other appointments in your life. The energy you get back will reward you many times over.

Now that you can create endless energy, what do you do with it? Unharnessed energy can be as detrimental as no energy at all. And that's why the next selling principle is just as important.

Your Sales Acceleration Steps

Step One: Make sleep a priority, by choosing a consistent daily bedtime and wake up time. Decide when you will wake up to do your *Miracle Morning*, and then back your way into a bedtime. Ensure that you are getting enough sleep and maintain a specific bedtime for a couple weeks to get your body on a natural clock. After a couple of weeks, feel free to play with the number of hours you leave for sleeping to optimize your energy levels. (Try nighttime sleep meditations if you struggle with getting to bed on time.)

Step Two: Incorporate time into your daily calendar to rest and recharge. For example, Hal takes a two-hour lunch break every day of the week, which gives him time to play basketball—something he loves to do and that reenergizes him. What can you plan in your day that will reenergize you? Outside your *Miracle Morning* routine, schedule regular daily periods to rest and recharge.

Step Three: Also plan your relaxation time for longer periods of time, such as a weekly date night, a monthly overnight getaway, or an annual vacation. Many of us have cycles in our sales calendar, and we should plan our life cycles around them. Schedule at least a couple weeks of vacation throughout the year, possibly even once a quarter. Schedule it (and pay for it) ahead of time, so you will force yourself to take it.

Step Four: Start eating for energy. Try incorporating one new healthy meal into your diet each day. If you already have one healthy meal, try adding a second or try some new healthy snacks. And remember to keep water with you at all times so that you stay hydrated.

Advanced Step: Find ways to combined multiple practices. Plan a hike with friends or family, or build a date night around preparing a healthy meal together.

TOP ONE PERCENT SALESPERSON INTERVIEW
John Ruhlin – CEO, The Ruhlin Group

John holds a place in history as the #1 distributor in the 65-year history of Cutco Cutlery, the largest US-made cutlery manufacturer in North America and one of the largest direct sales companies in the world. Although record-breaking sales results are what have given him a platform, he is the founder of *The Ruhlin Group*, a company that specializes in helping companies develop and execute year round strategic gifting and appreciation programs for prospects, employees, clients, investors, and other key stakeholders.

"I have two kids, so my morning wake up time varies a little bit. It depends on travelling overseas or otherwise, but it averages between 5:30 and 6:00. I get up and get my contacts in immediately to help get my eyes awake. I get a glass of water. I try to get protein in me as soon as possible, whether it's four or five eggs or some leftover chicken from the night before. Then I get a handful of nuts and a handful of berries. I have a sauna down in my home office, so I will go down there and do some breathing exercises, or I would go to the gym. I either do some cardio or the special strength training program that I am part of right now. If I don't get my exercise in during my morning, then it becomes a lot harder as the day goes on."

"I get in some devotional time. Typically, I read the Bible for 10 minutes or so, and then pray for 10 minutes or so as well. I also try to read for another 15–30 minutes throughout the day whether it's the *Wall Street Journal* or *Business Insider*. Often I am just pulling it up on my phone to keep current on business events or just current events."

"When I was younger, I could just work longer and more hours. I could stay up till two or three in the morning to get things done. But, as more priorities and more important priorities have come into my life, I have realized that if I don't have that set plan and priorities for the first part of the day, it's a roll of the dice if

I am going to get anything productive done that day. Overall, I think getting a workout in, even if the day falls apart, you can say at least I took care of myself and got this done. I think from a confidence perspective, people feel better and more confident when they feel strong physically and mentally, which comes from things like working out and prayer."

MIRACLE MORNING SUCCESS STORY
Albert Belo – Founder, Million Miracles for Kids

"I have always woken up early in the morning in order to go to work but it was often a struggle. I hated getting out of bed, no longer enjoyed what I did for a living and felt tired all the time.

"TMM has transformed my life so much! I wake up early very regularly, sometimes even before my alarm goes off. I feel energized throughout the day and accomplish so much more. My productivity and clarity has improved tremendously.

"I used to work for a company and didn't like what I was doing, before TMM. Now I am not only with another company that I enjoy working with, I am also in a partner/entrepreneur role and have been able to increase my income by 15%."

— 6 —

Not-So-Obvious Selling Principle #3:

UNWAVERING FOCUS

*"Successful people maintain a positive focus in life
no matter what is going on around them. They stay
focused on their past successes rather than their pas
failures, and on the next action steps they need to
take to get them closer to the fulfillment of their
goals, rather than all of the other distractions that
life presents to them."*
—JACK CANFIELD

We've all met that person. You know—*that* person. The one who runs marathons, coaches little league, volunteers at her son's school lunch program, cooks great meals, and maybe writes a memoir on the side. And on top of all that? She's an incredible salesperson, topping the charts at her office, or knocking it out of the park when it comes to growing her business.

I bet you know someone like that—someone who just seems amazingly productive. What you might not realize, though, is exactly how they do it. Maybe you always thought they were lucky. Or gifted. Or connected. Or had the right personality. Or were born with superpowers!

While those things can help when it comes to sales, I know from experience that the real superpower behind every unbelievably productive salesperson is *focus*.

Focus is the ability to maintain clarity on your highest priorities, then take all that endless energy you've learned to generate for yourself and zero it in on what matters most, and keep it there, regardless of what is going on around you, or how you feel.

When you harness the power of focus, you don't become superhuman, but you can achieve seemingly superhuman results. And the reasons why are surprisingly straightforward:

- **Focus makes you more effective.** Being effective doesn't mean to do the most things or to do things the fastest. It means to do the *right* things. You engage in the activities that move the needle in your business and generate sales.

- **Focus makes you more efficient.** Being efficient means to do things with the least amount of resources, like time, energy or money. Every time your mind wanders away from your work, you waste those things—particularly time. In sales, time is money so every moment that your focus wavers is another dollar (or thousands of dollars) lost.

- **Focus makes you productive**. When you focus on your highest priorities, do the right things, and do them in the right way, you get more done, with less effort. Too often we confuse being *busy*—engaged in activities that don't produce sales, like cleaning your car or reorganizing your leads for the 12th time this month—with being productive. By taking the steps that we're about to cover, you'll learn how to develop the habit of unwavering focus and join the ranks of the most productive salespeople in the world.

Combine those benefits, and it results in your selling and earning a *lot* more. Perhaps the greatest value of focus, however, is that it moves the needle not just on the sales chart, but also in every important area of your life. Rather than scattering your energy across multiple areas and getting mediocre results across the board, focus releases your untapped selling potential *and* improves your life.

Now let's turn your *Miracle Morning* to the task. Here are the three steps you need to turn your morning time into laser focused, super-productive time.

1. Find Your Best Environment(s) to Focus.

Let's start here: *You need an environment that supports your commitment to unwavering focus.* It might be your sales office, your home office, or it could be a coffee shop. No matter how modest, though, you need a place where you go to focus on conducting business.

Part of the reason for this is simple logistics. If your work is scattered from the trunk of your car to the kitchen counter, you simply can't be effective. A bigger reason, however, is that **having a place where you focus triggers the habit of focusing**. Trying to work at your kitchen table or make sales calls while sitting on your living room couch leaves you susceptible to being pulled into non-productive activities, like grabbing a bite to eat or watching television. Sit at the same desk and do great work at the same time every day, and soon enough you'll find yourself slipping into the zone just by sitting down.

If you're on the road a lot, like me, then your car, your suitcase, and possibly random coffee shops are part of your focus space, too. Build habits for how you pack and work on the road, and you can trigger great focus in the same way you do at the office. Being able to work anywhere can become a bonus when you are prepared and always have with you exactly what you need. I could even come and work on your couch or guestroom if necessary (just waiting on that invitation).

2. Clear the Clutter

Stuff is a focus killer, and it's our next stop on the journey. There are two kinds of clutter, mental and physical, and we all have them both. There are the things we carry around in our minds that need to be done, such as, *my sister's birthday is coming up. I have to get her a gift and card.* Or *I had a great time at dinner the other night,*

I need to send the host a thank you note. Or *I have to answer the email from my new client before I leave the office today.*

And there are things we carry around in our physical lives. Stacks of paper. Old magazines. Sticky notes. Clothes we never wear. The pile of junk in the garage. The trinkets, knick-knacks, and tokens that accumulate as we go through life.

Clutter of either type creates the equivalent of a heavy fog, and to become focused, you need to be able to *see*. To clear your vision, you'll want to get those mental items out of your head and collected so you can relieve the mental stress of trying to remember them. And then, you'll want to get those physical items out of your way.

Here's a simple process to help you clear the fog and create the clarity you need to focus.

- **Create a master to-do list**. You probably have lots of things that haven't been written down yet–start with those. And all those tiny little sticky notes that clutter your desk, computer screen, day timer, countertops, on the refrigerator … Are there other places? Put those notes and action items on your master list. Put them all into one central location, whether that's a physical journal or a list on your phone, so that you can completely clear your mental storage. Feeling better? Keep going, it gets better.

- **Purge your workspace.** Schedule a half (or full) day to go through every single stack of paper, file folder with documents to be filed in other folders, trays full of unopened mail … You get the gist. Throw out or shred what you don't need. Scan and/or file the ones that matter. Note in your journal any items that need your attention, that you cannot delegate, and pick a time in your schedule to complete them.

- **Declutter your life.** Clean up and clear out every drawer, closet, cabinet, and trunk that doesn't give you a sense of calm and peace when you see it. This includes your car. This could take a few hours or a few days. Schedule a short time each day until everything is complete. Saying, "I just need a weekend to declutter," is a sure way to never start. Pick a single *drawer*, and start there.

Getting physically and mentally organized will allow you to focus at a level you would never believe possible. It leaves your energy nowhere to go except to what *matters*.

3. Build Unwavering Focus

Once you identify your focus place, and begin the process of decluttering your life, you should experience a remarkable increase in focus simply from clearing the fog in your mind.

Now, it's time to take things to the next level. I use three questions to improve my focus every day. They are:

- What's working that **I should *keep* doing** (or do more of)?
- What do **I need to *start* doing** to accelerate results?
- What do **I need to immediately *stop* doing** that's holding me back from going to the next level?

If you can answer those three questions, and take action on the answers, you'll discover a whole new level of productivity you might not have thought was even possible. Let's look at each question in detail.

What Do You Need to *Keep* Doing (or do more of)?

Let's face it: not all sales tactics and strategies are created equal. Some work better than others. Some work for a period of time and then become less effective. Some make things worse!

Right now, you're probably doing a lot of the right activities, and you'll be nodding right along as you read the coming chapters on the best practice sales techniques. If you already know there are things you're doing that are working, jot those down. Perhaps you're constantly prospecting and finding potential customers, for example. Put that on the "what's working" list. Perhaps a networking group is delivering great leads—add that to the list, too.

Make sure you're choosing things that are actually contributing to increasing your sales. Consider the 80/20 rule (originally the Pareto principle), proving time and time again that roughly 80 percent of our results come from 20 percent of our efforts. Which

20 percent of your activities impact 80 percent of your results? It's easy to keep the things that you *like* doing, but this is sales—you need to make sure that the activities you're doing are directly related to producing leads, closing deals, and putting money in your bank account.

At the end of this chapter, you'll have an opportunity to capture in your journal the activities that are working. (Among them, I hope, will be that you've started doing the Life S.A.V.E.R.S. to take your personal development to the next level.) Everything that's on that list is a "keep doing" until it's replaced by something even more effective.

For all of the keep doing activities on your list, make sure you're completely honest with yourself about *what you need to be doing more of* (aka *what you're currently not doing enough of*). Are you averaging 20 prospecting calls per day, but haven't been reaching your sales goals? Remember: **any percentage that you increase your prospecting process, over an extended period of time, will result in that same percentage of an increase in your sales**. Go from 20 calls a day to 30 calls a day (a 50percent increase), and it will only be a matter of time before you see your sales increase by roughly 50 percent.

Keep doing what's working, depending on how much more you want to sell, simply do that much *more* of what's working.

What Do You Need to *Start* Doing?

Once you've captured what's working—and determined what's working *that you need to do more of*—it's time to decide what *else* you can do that will accelerate your success.

I have a few top-shelf suggestions to prime the pump and get you started:

- Organize your database for targeted follow up and lead generation with past clients, current prospects, and your sphere of influence, so that you can consistently generate a stream of repeat sales and ongoing referrals. For comprehensive training on this topic, we highly recommend Michael J. Maher's bestselling book, *The 7 Levels of Communication*.

- Make sure your online presence is driving business. You can either use a service like *Likeable Hub* (likeablehub.com) or hire someone to optimize your social media accounts and to improve SEO, conversion rates, and content development.

- Create your *Foundational Schedule*—a recurring, ideal weekly schedule with a time-blocked calendar, so that every day when you wake up, your highest priorities are already predetermined and planned. Then, make any necessary adjustments on Sunday night for the following week.

- Review your marketing pieces to ensure they are targeting the right audience. Are they pointing to your target prospects' needs and wants and highlighting solutions you offer?

- Once you've identified which activities you're spending time on that do *not* directly impact your sales, plan your first hire (or your next hire). This could be a personal assistant, a virtual assistant, or an intern, to save some cash. Realize that hiring someone to free up your time is an *investment*, not an expense. What would it be worth for you to free up enough of your time for you to increase your sales by 20–50percent? It's time for you to start thinking bigger.

I caution you to not become overwhelmed here. Keep in mind that Rome wasn't built in a day. You don't need to identify 58 action items and implement them by tomorrow. The great news about having a daily scribing (aka journaling) practice means that you can capture everything. Then, one-by-one or two-by-two, add them to your success arsenal until they become habits.

What Do You Need to *Stop* Doing?

By now you've most likely added a few items to start doing. If you're wondering where the time is going to come from, this might be the best step of all. It's time to let go of some of the things you've been doing up until now that don't serve you in order to make room for ones that do.

I'm fairly sure there are a number of daily activities you will be relieved to stop doing, thankful to delegate to someone else, or grateful to not have to do.

Why not stop

- eating unhealthy, energy-draining foods that suck the life and motivation out of you?
- working when you're tired and on the weekends and holidays?
- replying to texts and emails instantly?
- answering the phone? Let it go to voicemail and reply when the timing works best for you.
- doing repetitive tasks such as paying the bills, buying groceries several times a week, or even cleaning your house?

Or, if you want to dramatically improve your focus in one simple step, then try this easy fix:

Stop responding to buzzes and sounds like a trained seal.

Do you really need to be notified when you receive texts, emails, and social media notifications? Nope, didn't think so. Go into the settings of your phones, tablets and computers and turn all of your notifications to the OFF setting.

Technology exists for your benefit, and you can take control of it this very minute. How often you check your phone messages, texts and email can and should be directed by *you*. Let's face it, we're salespeople, not emergency room physicians. We don't need to be accessible and instantly responding to others 24/7/365. An effective alternative is scheduling times throughout the day to check in on what's happening, what needs your immediate attention, what items can be added to your schedule or master to do list, and also what can be deleted, ignored, and/or forgotten.

When I was an agent, my voicemail message let people know that I would check my voicemail at noon and 4:00 p.m. If it were an emergency, they should text me at this same number. By setting proper expectations around response times, clients were never disappointed when it took me a few hours to get back to them. In fact, unless they texted me, they were accepting the fact that their call did not require immediate attention.

Unwavering Focus is a Habit

Focus is like a muscle that you build over time. And, like a muscle, you need to show up and do the work to make it grow. Cut yourself some slack if you falter, but keep pushing forward. It will get easier. It might take you time to learn to focus, but every day that you try, you'll continue to get better at it. Ultimately, this is about *becoming* someone who focuses, which starts with seeing yourself as such. I recommend that you add a few lines to your affirmations about your commitment to unwavering focus and what you will do each day to develop it.

Most salespeople would be shocked to discover just how little time they spend on truly important, sales-relevant activities each day. Today, or in the next 24 hours, schedule 60 minutes to focus on the *single most important sales task you do*, and you'll be amazed not only by your productivity, but also by how empowering it feels.

By now, you've added some pretty incredible action items and focus areas to your salesperson's success arsenal. After you complete the steps below, head into the next section where we will sharpen your sales skills combined with the Life S.A.V.E.R.S. in ways you might not have heard or thought of before!

Your Sales Accelerator Steps

Step One: Free your mind with a brain dump. Unload all those little to-do lists floating around in your head. Create a master to-do list in your journal.

Step Two: Build your Three Unwavering Focus lists:

- What I need to keep doing (or do more of)
- What I need to start doing
- What I need to stop doing

Step Three: For the next week, keep a list of all the things you spend time doing and how long you spent on each task. What can be automated, outsourced, or delegated? How much time did you spend on your top sales/income-producing activities? Repeat this process until you are clear on what your *process* is, and start time-blocking your days so that you're spending as close to close to 80 percent of your time on tasks that produce results. Delegate the rest.

Finally, remember to start implementing Hal's not-so-obvious secret to sales success: *commit to your process without being emotionally attached to your results.*

TOP ONE PERCENT SALESPERSON INTERVIEW
Pat Petrini, Owner, P&E Properties, LLC

Pat Petrini was kind enough to spend some time letting us interview him about his more than 12 years and $25 million in sales ranging from direct sales to network marketing. Pat was the youngest person to reach the rank of Premier Distributor with Xango and was selected as one of the Top Mentors in the direct-selling industry by BusinessForHome.org. In reviewing Pat's interview, I found that his efficiency and focus has been a clear advantage in his continued successes.

"We have 24 hours in each day. The difference between the most successful people (no matter how you define success) and everybody else is the cumulative effect of how they chose to spend those 24 hours."

Pat goes onto explain how his daily routines help him focus efficiently on his most important tasks: "My morning generally starts with a protein shake and a CrossFit workout. After the workout, shower, and breakfast, I usually have a prioritized list of tasks that I have selected the night before that I will attempt to accomplish throughout the day in between appointments. The most important tasks are prioritized first, and *important* tasks are those that move me towards my long-term goals. The urgent tasks are prioritized later; *urgent* tasks are those that have an upcoming deadline. Always prioritize important tasks over urgent tasks. The urgent tasks might help you get through the week, but the important tasks will ultimately determine what your life will look like five years from now."

MIRACLE MORNING SUCCESS STORY
Erica Hageman–Owner, RE/MAX Momentum

"Before *The Miracle Morning*, I was a morning hater. My snooze button was my friend—my BFF really."

As a wife and mom to two young daughters, trying to manage a busy and growing real estate office meant high blood pressure, high stress levels, and being overwhelmed. Now, Erica is a fan of all of the Life S.A.V.E.R.S., each being special in its own way.

"I can see a huge difference the days I do the Life S.A.V.E.R.S. I tend to be more calm and focused."

Like with most people, adopting *The Miracle Morning* as a habit is a work in progress, but worth the extra effort it takes. Erica said, "I will have eighty-five agents in my organization by the end of the year, which is up by twenty. We will be talking with HQ about our fourth franchise purchase. I will have closed thirty sales (this is my personal business on top of running RE/MAX Momentum). I will be down my final ten pounds, Momentum will close over $240,000,000 in 2014. This is all possible and will happen! Check, check, double check as it is up to me as the leader of my life and Momentum. *The Miracle Morning* gives me clarity that I just can't find any other way. It's so refreshing to start the day on a calm, inspiring note."

— 7 —

SALES ACCELERATION SKILL #1:

ATTRACTING LEVEL 10 CUSTOMERS

"Pretend that every single person you meet has a sign around his or her neck that says, 'Make me feel important.' Not only will you succeed in sales, you will succeed in life."

—MARY KAY ASH, Founder, Mary Kay Cosmetics

Imagine you're just a few yards from the finish line of an important sale.

You've worked hard on this one. You're emotionally invested. You've put in the time, money and resources it takes to shepherd someone from lead to prospect to customer. You've answered every question dealt with every objection, and bent over backwards to help them make the right decision. And now, at last, you're basking in the anticipation of what is a sure thing—in your mind, you've already got your commission spent.

And then at the last minute they decide *not* to buy.

It's a crushing disappointment ... at first. But before long, you've managed to console yourself that it just wasn't your fault. *Oh well,* you tell yourself. *They just weren't ready.* Or, *they bought from my competition.* Or, *they didn't have the money.* And then you head home to lick your wounds.

In these situations, it can be easy to reframe failure and attribute the lost sale to something out of your control. But whatever the reason you tell yourself, there's a good chance the real culprit is something you haven't considered:

You were selling to the wrong prospect.

It's the first key of successful sales, and the one most often overlooked. You can blame the economy, the prospect, the competition, the banks, the product, the marketing team, the manufacturer, or any number of other people. But often, the truth is right there: *you invested time in the wrong person.*

Level 10 Customers

Now think back to a time when you made a sale that seemed almost effortless. The person was responsive. Your product or service truly helped, and was a perfect fit. They were delighted that you even *approached* them, and were even more thrilled when they put your product or service to work. They couldn't wait to buy. And refer. The whole sales process, from first contact to close, was seamless and fast.

How did that feel? My guess is: *outstanding.* I bet you left that sale thinking, "If every sale was like that, I'd be the greatest salesperson on the planet."

But what if every sale *could* be like that?

It can. Because the reason that sale went so smoothly and left you feeling like the rockstar you truly are isn't that you were on your game, in the zone, or rocking your mojo. *It's because you were working with a Level 10 customer.* Unlike the sale that went poorly, this sale was effortless and successful because you chose the right prospect.

A Level 10 customer is someone who needs what you have, needs it soon, and can afford to pay for it. They're the kind of person who falls in love with your product or service, and bends over backward to tell their network about it. They have the authority, the desire, and the ability to buy what you offer. They're responsive, interested and easy to work with.

Does that seem like a tall order?

In fact, it *is* a tall order. And that's exactly the type of order you need to make to reach your sales potential.

Qualifying: Mining for Level 10 Gold

Not everyone is your customer.

Repeat that to yourself as often as you need to in order to wire it into your brain and belief system. *Not everyone is your customer.* In fact, for some salespeople, it may be that hardly *anyone* is your customer. But those that are? They're Level 10, and they're going to transform your sales career.

But which ones are they, and how to do you find—or attract—them? Your prospects aren't walking the streets wearing "Level 10" t-shirts. You have to identify them by *qualifying* them.

No, you can't know for sure if the person in front of you is going to buy. But you can do your best to make sure they're an ideal fit.

You might feel it a challenge to spend the time and energy necessary to qualify your prospects, but here are six key reasons I hope will convince you to be rigidly intentional when qualifying your prospects *before* you invest in them:

1. Qualifying ensures that you only work with people who are really going to buy.

Qualifying helps you determine *if* your prospect is going to buy and more importantly, *when*. Are they going to buy now? Can they buy at all? What needs to happen before they are willing or able to buy? Are they just gathering information for a purchase that may be months or years down the road? Perhaps they like to look, yet never intend to buy. By qualifying, you avoid wasting resources on prospects that inevitably do nothing.

2. Qualifying tells you where to focus.

All that work you've done to build your powers of focus? It all goes to waste if you focus on someone who won't buy. You have a finite amount of time and energy—you must determine which prospects deserve it. Qualifying helps you to identify the highest probability opportunities to zero in on, so you can walk away from the rest.

3. Qualifying increases your closing rate.

When you only sell to prospects that are going to buy, you increase your probability of success. That means you need far fewer prospects to make the same number of sales, and you can spend more time cashing checks and less time prospecting.

4. Qualifying speeds up your sales and shortens the sales cycle.

Qualifying reveals the pain or pleasure points that can encourage your prospect to act now, instead of six months from now. Get curious about your clients and ask lots of questions. When you discover your prospect's compelling need, you can use your super sales power to help them make an informed buying decision more quickly.

5. Qualifying reduces your costs.

Time is money. Brochures, business cards, and collateral materials all cost money—even digital materials have a cost. If you routinely attempt to sell to people who have a low probability of purchasing, or simply are not going to buy ever, then you are ultimately wasting more time, money, and energy than you need to.

6. Qualifying gets you the best customers and clients.

Have you ever had a client you wish wasn't your client? (Perhaps you have one now?)

Challenging clients require so much time and energy that you could argue that they're *not worth having*. If you are constantly having to collect from, convince, or defend pain-in-the-you-know-what clients, you understand the phrase, "You earn every dime twice." These clients not only have a high aggravation factor, they distract you from finding and serving your ideal Level 10 clients. That alone means they cost you more money than they deliver. Qualifying can help make sure every single person you do business with in the future will be someone you enjoy working with.

Qualifying is About Two Things

As salespeople, we have a tendency to want to close every deal. We want to help every lead buy our product or service. We must learn that every time we say "yes" to something, we are saying "no" to something else. When we spin our wheels with an unqualified prospect we are saying "no" to the qualified client we could be speaking with instead.

No matter how hard you work or how many hours you put in, the great benefits of working with Level 10 customers will remain just out of reach if you aren't willing to qualify potential customers.

Fortunately, that process isn't as hard as it sounds. Qualifying is really about two things: *deciding what a Level 10 customer looks like* and *saying no to everyone else.*

The Life S.A.V.E.R.S.—Your Qualifying Connection

Qualifying, much like its close relative, prospecting, is as much a mental game as any other part of the sales process. Although each practice of the Life S.A.V.E.R.S. factors into your qualifying success, there are three you can use, almost to an unfair advantage, over your fellow salespeople and competitors: *silence, affirmations*, and *visualization.*

Spending time in silence has many benefits, which I have shared in earlier sections. The clarity that you gain from silence contribute to your sales success for one simple reason: a calm, centered sales-person is an extremely *likeable* salesperson. Unlike your colleagues, you won't reek of desperation. You won't be vibrating with frantic energy. Your tranquil demeanor will amplify your authenticity and attract qualified buyers to you like bees to honey. If you add any descriptive words to your practice of silence, add tranquil, calm, and centered to the list, because they will serve you quite well.

I also encourage you to create your own compelling affirmations specifically around qualifying prospects, especially if in the past you have wasted significant amounts of time with people who didn't buy from you. An affirmation like: *Every day, I attract, seek out, and only invest my valuable time with highly qualified prospects that have the need, desire, and ability to buy from me.*

Like your affirmations, your visualization practice needs to include a specific mini-movie in which you picture yourself enthusiastically connecting with qualified prospects. See yourself sitting across from someone who comes into your store, nodding and smiling as you ask pointed questions about their reason for talking with you. Picture them thumbing through your brochure, nodding, smiling, and then handing over their credit card to make the purchase.

Using the power of the Life S.A.V.E.R.S. in this way will not only help you to attract more prospects, but also you'll attract the *right* ones. And that will lead to a totally transformed sales career.

Now that you have a clear vision of qualifying using *The Miracle Morning* edge, let's get on with the business of finding those Level 10 customers. It's time to get you out there prospecting like the star you are!

Prospecting: Finding Your Level 10 Customers

Prospecting is the lifeblood of any successful salesperson's career. A sale is closed only after it is successfully *opened*, and the best salespeople focus their energy, in part, toward consistently opening new relationships.

Successful prospecting is truly an art, but it's an art you can learn, practice, master, and make your own. Because prospecting is built on self-discipline, which rests squarely on the shoulders of personal growth, anyone can master it. The more you work on yourself, the better you will be, both as a person, and as a prospector. Being great at prospecting isn't only about what you do. It's also about who you're being while you're doing it!

I believe that great prospecting finds its roots in the six disciplines of the Life S.A.V.E.R.S. Use them, and you will have all the energy, charisma, self-confidence, and determination you need to successfully seek and find prospects. As you sharpen your skills, you will easily attract more and more customers, almost as if by magic.

Let's take a look at the four key areas of effective prospecting: *Who, Where, How,* and *How Often.*

1. WHO: Identify Your Level 10 Customer

Do you know exactly who your ideal client is? You should be able to list at least the five basic characteristics of your ideal client or customer. For example:

1. Professional service provider in a senior-level position

2. Between the ages of 35 and 55

3. Income in excess of $250,000 per year

4. Lives in zip code 90210

5. Has a credit score above 720

If you can't list at least five characteristics, you won't get very far very fast, if ever. If you don't have a clear target, try this: think of three of your favorite current clients, and note several of their qualities and characteristics. That should get you started in figuring out the profile of your ideal prospect.

Put this list where you can see it every day. Memorize it. Create an avatar out of it. This avatar is the profile of the Level 10 customer you want to attract when you are prospecting.

This Level 10 customer must become your new *standard,* for which you will accept nothing less. Realize that it takes just as much time, effort, and energy to spend time with the wrong ones as it does the right ones. One could argue that nothing has the power to skyrocket your sales more than making the shift to relentlessly qualifying your prospects.

Attracting Level 10 customers starts with knowing exactly who your Level 10 customer is.

2. WHERE: How to Find Your Level 10 Customers

When new agents start working with me, one of the first questions I hear is, "Where do I find prospective buyers and sellers?" It's a valid question, to be sure. It can seem overwhelming to find the people who are ready to engage, buy, or sell at just the right time.

Whether you are a brand new salesperson or a top performer, I recommend you expand your list of prospects from the following sources, in this order:

- **Circle of Influence.** Do you realize that there are already dozens (and possibly hundreds) of people in your current network that would buy from you and refer you to their contacts? Start by making a list of everyone you know, even if you've only met them once or haven't seen them for 10 years. In fact, here's a little ninja tip: Rather than being afraid to call someone that you don't know very well or haven't seen in a long time, use that exact fact as the reason for calling them. "Hey _____, we haven't had a chance to get to spend much time together, but I've heard great things about you from _____. When would be a good time to get together for lunch, or even coffee?"

- **Referrals.** The legendary sales trainer Jim Rohn often preached that "referrals are the most important aspect of your business. Without them, there is no future." I've got to agree with Jim on this one. Your future sales, income, and success will be largely determined by how effective you are getting your customers to give you referrals.

Think of referrals as your potential income. The more referrals you have to call on, the more potential income is available to you, just waiting for you to make the calls and claim it. In the next chapter, we'll give you the exact steps, including what to say and when to say it, to create an endless supply of qualified referrals.

- **Professional Networks.** Leverage local networking groups, associations, and clubs to meet new prospects and generate ongoing referrals. During Hal's best year in sales, he joined a local *LeTip* business-networking group. By the end of the year, more than five percent of his sales were made to his fellow members and their referrals.

The key to successful networking is to focus on adding as much value as you can to each person and group, rather than doing what most salespeople do, which is looking to extract as much value as they can. *The more value you add to the lives of others, the more valuable you become, and the more value you attract.* Focus on developing a reputation as someone who is always striving to give more value than you ask for in return.

Here are some of the top networking groups for you to search for, and consider joining, in your area:

- **BNI** (www.bni.com)
- **LeTip** (www.letip.com)

- **Online Sources.** From the crucial role that email marketing plays in your customer relationships management to maximizing your online brand through the seemingly infinite number of social media sites like Twitter, Facebook, Google+, LinkedIn, Instagram, Pinterest, and more, many old school sales lead generation techniques are being replaced, enhanced, or automated by technology. Just like the key to successful networking, shared previously, the key to online success is to focus on adding value. When your emails and online posts consistently add value for others, you become valuable to them. Over time, you'll develop your personal brand as someone of value, rather than someone who is always trying to sell something to others.

  - For a comprehensive training on effective mail marketing, we recommend the book, *Email Persuasion* by Ian Brodie.
  - For a comprehensive training on maximizing your social media efforts, we recommend the book, *Jab, Jab, Jab, Right Hook* by Gary Vaynerchuk.

- For a comprehensive training on the maximizing the number one social media site *for business*, LinkedIn, we recommend the book, *Ultimate Guide to LinkedIn for Business (Ultimate Series)* by Ted Prodromou.

- **Purchased Lists.** While this can be an effective way to target prospects that fit your ideal demographic or have the job title that typically buy your offering, this is the last strategy we recommend. Selling is about relationships, and you have no relationship with the prospects on a purchased list. Think of it this way: who is more likely to buy from you, a person who you've been referred to by someone they know, like, and trust ... or a prospect who received a cold call from you? Purchased lists should definitely be considered as one part of your overall prospecting strategy, but we don't recommend it as the frontrunner.

For example, my agents and I use MLS real estate listings to find expired listings—properties that didn't sell during their listing—and then have one of our administrative staff narrow down the list by eliminating homes that have sold since they expired. Then they gather workable contact information for the remaining viable leads. In real estate, as with most industries, different tools exist for prospecting lists. We use the Cole Resource Directory paired with the Do Not Call list to scrub for home and cell phone numbers of entire neighborhoods that we are working. To find FSBO (For Sale By Owner) and expired leads there are sources like Mojo and RedX.

For sphere of influence, consider going through your Facebook friends as a place to start. In business-to-business sales, often a yellow pages will suffice, or a directory from your local Chamber of Commerce. Spend a little time reaching out to leaders in your industry and find out what is working for them. There is no need to reinvent the wheel. I suggest you identify the system that helps you to easily know where you are in the process of each relationship.

3. HOW: Become a Level 10 Person to Attract Level 10 Clients

Regardless of what you say or do, nothing determines how people (or prospects) respond to you more than *who you are*. This is another place your Life S.A.V.E.R.S. are going to impact your results.

Have you ever met someone who looked right, had the right things to say, and was even selling a great product, yet you didn't resonate with him or her, and you couldn't figure out why? Me too. Quite often, in fact!

An invisible yet unstoppable key to success is to make yourself irresistible to others. If you feel like you do everything right and yet there's a block in business flowing to you, chances are the issue lies, not with what you are doing, but *how you are being*. It's critical to be likable and approachable.

The best way to become a likable, approachable salesperson is to rock your Life S.A.V.E.R.S. every morning. It's the gateway to having a magnetic personality, complete with unstoppable attitude and an irresistible energy.

When you begin each day with a period of **Silence**, you create a sense of peace within, which improves your emotional intelligence and allows you to interact with people in a much more calm and thoughtful manner. You'll notice that most people who meditate each day have lower levels of stress and are less reactive and more intentional in all of their interactions. Thus, they tend to be more likeable and trustworthy. On the other hand, the average salesperson is highly stressed, reactive and overly emotional, and can't always be trusted to make the best decisions.

As time spent in silence creates a calm, focused internal environment, following it with **Affirmations** allows you to articulate (in writing) your vision for *the person you are committed to becoming*—your Level 10 self—so that you can be present to living in alignment with your vision, every day. By clearly defining the mindset, habits, and actions that you aspire to embody, and reading them every day, you will accelerate how quickly your vision becomes a reality.

Finally, your affirmations should be followed by **Visualization**—seeing and experiencing yourself being the person that you've just affirmed. Make sure that when you visualize, you *feel* what your vision will feel like. The effectiveness of visualization without congruent feelings is limited. For example, if you visualize yourself confidently presenting to prospects, be sure to generate *feelings* of confidence. You can also visualize people being drawn to you and wanting to know about you and what you're selling.

We recommend revisiting and rereading chapter 3 to deepen your learning around each of the Life S.A.V.E.R.S. While any of these six practices might only take a few minutes to learn, each of them can truly take a lifetime to master.

Level 10 Integrity

Once you've turned on your magnetic personality and selling charisma, it's important to maintain impeccable integrity in your sales approach. Having a high-integrity approach and treating each prospect and customer as you would your best friend, mother, or grandmother is the foundation of, not only making sales, but also in creating a customer base of loyal, raving fans. This is the key to *long-term* success as a salesperson.

Maintaining integrity is especially important in sales. After all, people tend to naturally raise an eyebrow at a salesperson coming their way. If I could teach only one value to live by, it would be to live with the utmost integrity—to do the right thing at all times and in all circumstances, whether or not anyone is watching.

Your reputation—also known as your *personal brand*—will at some point begin preceding you, so always do everything in your power to make yours impeccable. If you wouldn't sell your products or service to your best friend, don't sell it to someone sitting across from you solely because they are willing to buy it. If it isn't right for them, do the right thing and don't let them buy it.

It takes courage to do the right thing, and in the short term it can be painful, but building a personal brand founded in integrity is a long-term success play. Remember: *how you show up today will affect where you end up tomorrow*, and for the rest of your life.

4. HOW OFTEN: The Power of Multiple Touches

Valuable relationships aren't built in a day, and sales aren't always closed during the first meeting. Your first connection with a prospect might be just the first step of many before you reach a sale, and it's important that you continue to move the relationship ahead.

Marketing experts teach that it takes seven touches over the course of sixty days to get the attention of a prospect. Our friend, Honorée Corder, teaches in her book *Business Dating: Applying Relationship Rules in Business for Ultimate Success* that every person has a number of times they need to be "touched" (contacted/connected with) and nobody knows what their number is! You simply have to be willing to be in a relationship with someone long enough to earn their trust, and through that, their business. You have to be willing to stay in the relationship until they buy from you, refer you, or die. Literally.

I advise you to design a system that allows you to consistently touch people and add value through email, phone calls, direct mail, newsletters, videos, podcasts, and any other way you can think of, as many times as necessary, until you build that trust. Some will buy on the first attempt, but most will only buy or engage after several touches. Your job is to just keep touching to build trust and rapport, and instill confidence in your prospect—confidence in both you and your product.

As famous sales and marketing trainer, Dan Kennedy says, "The Fortune is in the follow up." Follow the *Sales Accelerator Steps* at the end of this chapter to create your fortune building follow up strategy. I recommend that you schedule time to develop your strategy for what your multiple touches over the next 90 days will be. The first touch may be the initial phone call or brochure you send. The second touch could be a follow-up note, or a value-added email with your most recent e-newsletter. Decide on a list of logical touches and schedule those touches with each person that you're attempting to gain as a client.

Don't worry about achieving perfection, *just take action*. The magic happens on the other side of taking action, and eventually you'll find the perfect system that works best for your prospects. Remember: *you don't have to be great to get started, but you have to get started to be great.*

Consistency Counts: Prospect Daily!

I know from experience that inconsistent prospecting produces inconsistent sales and yields mediocre results. If you want serious success, it's critical to prospect daily for a minimum of five days a week. Prospecting is the *process* you must commit to each day (without being emotionally attached to your day-to-day results, of course).

There are two reasons why consistency is important: *momentum* and *expectation.*

There is power and psychological advantage in the momentum you gain from taking consistent, daily action. When you do something every day, it becomes, not only a habit, but a part of your identity. And while it takes motivation and effort to start a new daily habit, eventually keeping it going can feel almost effortless. You'll get to the point where *not* doing it doesn't feel right, because the daily action has become part of who you are.

As I write this book, I strive to write every single day—that's my *process* that I'm committed to. I do it every day. That means I don't have to start over after missing several days. There's no need to recalibrate, go back, and start again. Writing every single day allows me to capitalize on the momentum of the day before. Sales is the same—you will eventually, and then consistently, capitalize on the momentum you gain, but only when you prospect daily.

The Road to Level 10

You're not trying to sell to everyone, not even close. In fact you shouldn't be trying to sell to most people. With more than seven billion people on this planet, you aren't even attempting to sell to even one percent of them.

The sooner you recognize that you have a specific and ideal target customer, the more successful you'll be. There's no need to get stuck on any one individual, trying to convince them they must buy from you. There are plenty of people who are ready, right now, to buy what you're selling, and your job is to find them and only them. And, to do it as quickly and efficiently as possible.

If you want to be seen as a reliable, professional, and trustworthy sales professional for your clients, you need to set high sales and business standards and stick to them. Once you determine your daily prospecting process, consider it carved in stone. It isn't something you do when you feel like it. It's something you do daily, regardless of whether you feel like it or not. Remember these wise words from Hal: *Salespeople who only do what they feel like doing don't do much. To be successful, you must take action even when you don't feel like it, knowing that the action itself is what produces the motivation you need to follow through.* In other words, motivation doesn't create action; action creates motivation.

In Summary

When you are committed to becoming a Level 10 person, you start to attract Level 10 people—and Level 10 customers—into your life. This is why waking up and doing your *Miracle Morning* every day, and accelerating your personal development through the Life S.A.V.E.R.S. truly is the fast way to take your SELF and your SALES to the next level.

Now what? Well, every top salesperson has attained a level of mastery when it comes to their sales presentation. So, once you've implemented the following *Sales Accelerator Steps* to begin attracting Level 10 customers, we're going to introduce and guide you through *Miraculous Presenting*—creating a sales presentation that generates results so far beyond what most salespeople believe is possible, people might start viewing each of your results as, well … miraculous.

The Sales Accelerator Steps

Step 1: Make a list of 5-10 character traits that describe exactly who your Level 10 customers are. Think back to your best clients. What do you know about them? Attracting Level 10 customers starts with being crystal clear as to exactly whom your Level 10 customer is. Once completed, put this list up where you can see it, commit to its being your new standard for prospecting, and don't settle for anything less.

Step 2: List your top 50–150 prospects. Get out of your comfort zone and realize that there are hundreds of Level 10 customers in your current network, just waiting for you to identify and call them. Think of everyone you know—friends, family, current clients, your database, professionals that you do business with, and even previous prospects who liked your offering but the timing wasn't right when you first saw them. Start by making your list as long as possible, and qualify them later.

Step 3: Determine where you interact with your best prospects. What are your top two or three lead sources? Review your budget and calendar to determine if you are spending your time and money in the right places for prospecting. Reference the ***start doing*** list that you made in the previous chapter.

Step 4: Create a system for following up with and nurturing your database, both automated and manually, to constantly improve relationships with your customers and prospects. Include mass touches such as email, direct mail, and online advertising, and make sure to incorporate enough personal touches through handwritten notes, phone calls, and in-person visits. For the most comprehensive training on systematizing your follow up, our go-to book is *7L: The Seven Levels of Communication* by Michael J. Maher.

TOP ONE PERCENT SALESPERSON INTERVIEW
Michael J. Maher – Founder, REFERCO

Michael J. Maher is the author of *7L: The Seven Levels of Communication*. Having spent over 15 years in sales, Michael has earned over a million dollars in commissions in a single year. He prides himself on always bringing value to a relationship, and he has developed a system for generating referrals consistently. Michael explains the importance of give and take in four simple words: Give Generously. Receive Appreciatively.

"The Triangle of Trust, as explained in *7L: The Seven Levels of Communication*, is utilizing your existing relationships to get connected and eventually the introduction to the prospect or influential person. Borrow the trust from that relationship to start your own relationship with the new person. In one case, I wanted to meet the relocation director at a large corporation, so that we could handle their business. I had three of my clients who worked there email and call that person, and then two of my Ambassadors who are influential AND knew that person called her as well. At 4:00 p.m. that day, I called. She was very impressed. We met and we got the business."

Michael continually talks about getting in relationship with the right people. The focus has to be on what you bring to the prospect to help achieve their goals, not what they can do for you. "As long as you make it all about the best interest of the client, you will succeed. As soon as money or desperation leak into your decisions, you are doomed. Keep it all about them. Don't worry about the numbers; focus on the people. If you take care of the people, the numbers will take care of themselves."

MIRACLE MORNING SUCCESS STORY
Rob Broadwell – Client Partner, SAP

The Miracle Morning came along at just the right time for Rob. About to turn 50, and questioning his value and ability to succeed, he discovered and devoured the book.

"Before TMM, I dealt with a lot of self-doubt. Was I too old to go after my dreams? Am I trapped in a job/career where I have no real passion? How would I ever be able to push through and have my 'break through?'"

You may not have discovered that age is truly just a number. If so, the Life S.A.V.E.R.S. can be the catalyst to help you discover that, and so much more, just like Rob.

"I have stepped out of my comfort zone and trusted that what I was doing is right. I have the confidence I used to have, but channeled in a different way, and am able to focus on what matters and how to accomplish more in less time."

"I am helping more people get what they want, mentoring others to reach their success, and on June 16th, I start a new job with one of the largest software companies in the world in a position that is highly coveted in the industry."

SALES ACCELERATION SKILL #2:

MIRACULOUS PRESENTING

"There are only two ways to live your life. One is as though nothing is a miracle. The other is as though everything is a miracle."
—ALBERT EINSTEIN

I bet you've experienced a time when you knocked your sales presentation out of the park. A time when the sales experience was so amazing that you left, contract and check in hand, vibrating with a sense of joy, excitement, and accomplishment—feeling like you could sell just about anything, to anyone. It was a moment when all elements of presenting your offer came together beautifully.

Most salespeople end up seeing those moments as the result of good fortune—a lucky day in string of less fortunate ones. But the truth is that with a shift in your perspective and your approach, every presentation can progress as though buyer, product, and seller were meant to meet.

You can, in other words, *make* the stars align!

The *Miracle Morning* Approach to Presenting

It's quite possible you've already been given a proven sales presentation. From supplements and appliances, to cars and accounting services, companies spend thousands, if not millions, of dollars to develop the right presentation to help you get more business and close more deals.

But many companies don't provide the best training (or any training at all), and as many salespeople can testify, the perfect, million-dollar presentation—built for the masses by a marketing team, somewhere—often doesn't stand up in the field.

If, in the past, you have been inadequately prepared for the delivery of your presentation, then you've experienced the gut-wrenching feeling of realizing you may have missed a prime opportunity. It's time for that to end. This chapter will take you through the steps necessary for you to go from mediocre presenting and missed opportunities to miraculous presenting, at will.

Step 1: Learn It All

Step 2: Craft Your Presentation

Step 3: Practice and Rehearse

Step 4: Stand (or sit) and Deliver

Step 5: Post-Presentation Review

Step 1: Learn It All

Great sales presentations begin long before you ever meet a prospect. Even before they *create* a presentation, successful salespeople have built an incredible knowledge base around their product, their prospects, and their competition.

Preparation (or lack thereof) is immediately apparent to a savvy prospect. The more insight you have about what you're selling, and whom you're selling to, the more comfortable you'll feel, and the more effective you'll be as a salesperson.

There's no better way to be perceived as an expert than to *feel* like one, and the starting point to expert sales status is to know everything you possibly can about a) your product, b) your market, and c) your competition that is competing for your prospects dollars.

A) Know What You're Selling

Successful salespeople know their product or service inside and out—and they love it. They constantly try to learn more about their product, from the ground up. They ask questions of other salespeople and experts. They know everything about a widget from the raw material to the glue used on the price sticker. They know which problems their product solves, and which features to emphasize that matter most to their prospects. They know they're selling the steak *and* the sizzle, and the more they know, the better.

You are no exception. Become as familiar as possible with your product or service, from the history of the company to the people that work there. Knowing every detail doesn't mean you have to *share* every detail, but that one little piece of information might make all the difference to someone who cares.

More important still, the fact that you care enough to invest the time to know more than every other salesperson might be what matters most.

B) Know Your Customer

Sales is about solving problems. No customer ever bought a drill because they wanted a drill, they bought a drill because they wanted a hole. So why does your customer want to buy what you're selling?

Understand your customers' needs, wants, and desires and how they're relevant to your product or service. Are you able to solve their problem? Can you help them avoid a problem? How is your customer's life *better* the minute they have your solution?

To answer those questions you need to understand your customer. The best way to do that is to design discovery questions that uncover their needs, wants, and desires, such as the following:

- What brings you in today?
- Why are you interested in purchasing a new washer and dryer?
- What do you like/not like about your current vehicle?
- If you bought the perfect new home, describe the picture you

have in your head to me.

- What does the perfect solution look like?
- What's held you back from making this purchase in the past?

There are two keys here. The first is to *be genuinely curious.* If you actually care about discovering your client's needs, you will. The second is to *close your mouth and open your ears.* Ask your questions, and then focus on truly hearing the answers.

The questions aren't magical, but what you hear back might just be.

C) Know Your Competition

Knowing what you're selling and to whom will take you a long way, but remember, *you're not selling in a vacuum.* There are other salespeople with great products and services who are out there trying to do the same thing you are. Of course, they won't be as prepared as you are, but that's no reason to discount them.

You need as much information as possible about the competition. Many of the questions and objections you field from your prospects will be about what your competition offers, and how you're different. In order to give a meaningful presentation, you have to know what the other guy is doing—not so you can throw them under the bus, but so you'll appear more honest, knowledgeable, and thorough.

Study the competition's products so you understand their strengths and weaknesses. Then, do a comparison against what you are selling. Be honest, and thorough. When the prospect brings up specific points about the competition's product or services, you'll be ready with an answer that actually might win you the sale. There's no harm in acknowledging your competition and even what's great about them. You want to understand where you excel and be ready to share it without being defensive.

With most information just one Google search away (sorry Bing), your clients are more informed than ever about you and your competitors. Armed with knowledge, truth, and experience this creates an opportunity for you to become an expert and trusted advisor. Even choosing to explain why you choose to sell your product over your competitor's could go a long way in closing the sale by building a relationship based in trust.

A wonderful side benefit of building your knowledge is that selling becomes exciting—you won't be able to get enough of it! Expert-level knowledge strips away any fear about questions your customers might have and makes any conversation about your product or service comfortable. Learn enough, and you'll be among the enviable few who are able to effortlessly connect with your prospect, walk them through the features and benefits of what you're selling, and have them buy from you as if the entire idea was theirs, and theirs alone.

Step 2: Craft Your Presentation

When you feel you know enough to begin to assemble your pitch, it's time to create your miraculous presentation. Sales presentations typically include the following components:

Establish rapport and credibility

Identify the problem or need

Describe your solution

Emphasize the benefits

Present the price

Close the sale

Ask for referrals

You can draft your presentation in any form, but make sure you cover these seven parts. When the time comes to actually present (step c) you can then revise it to fit your style, your format, your customer, and your offering.

A) Establish rapport and credibility from the start, so your prospects like you and understand why listening to you is a good investment of their time and attention.

Many sales trainers will teach you old school techniques like asking your prospect about the "3 Ps"—people, pets, and plants.

Most Level 10 customers are savvier than your run of the mill prospects. Wasting their time with small talk is rarely the best strategy for establishing mutual trust, respect, and likeability. Instead, we recommend a much more direct approach that spends as little time as possible before you *get to the point.*

To quickly **establish rapport**, try an opening like this: "Mrs. Prospect, I know your time is valuable and I'd imagine you've probably got a lot of other things you could be doing right now, so I really want to thank you for taking the time to meet with me today. I don't want to waste any of your time, so to see if this [my product] is even a good fit for you, do you mind if I ask you a few questions?" This approach creates rapport, not through small talk, but through a mutual respect for one another's time.

Ultimately, rapport and trust are built throughout your entire presentation, not just in your opening. Many salespeople actually end up losing trust when they try to front load rapport into the beginning, causing it to feel forced and fake. Consider that if you are friendly, knowledgeable, and respectful throughout your presentation, you will build much stronger rapport with your customers than if you force questions about their dog, Rover, and that Picasso hanging over their fireplace.

To **establish credibility**, leverage your clients' results more than your own. While you can talk about how credible you are until you're blue in the face, gathering case studies in the form of written testimonials from your customers will show how you've got experience helping people who are just like them. And if you *haven't* worked with someone just like them? Take the time to talk to other salespeople in your company to find testimonials for your product, which you can use in your presentations.

Be careful to not come off like you're trying too hard to impress your prospect. This typically makes you come across as insecure. Instead, focus only on essentials relevant to the prospect that enhance your credibility.

B) Identify the problem or need facing your prospect. If you're selling a $250,000 sports car to a bachelor in his 30s, he most likely wants status and speed. If you're selling a starter home to a couple expecting their first baby, they want space, safety, and security. A business owner may need to save time or money. You can develop different statements that address the needs of your typical customer, but also the needs of a specific customer that you know you'll be sitting in front of at your next meeting.

Resist the urge to get into the features of your product or service at this stage. This is all about the need of the person in front of you. This needs analysis stage provides a great opportunity to build more rapport as you learn more about your client and listen for areas where your product or service can solve their problem. This is your opportunity to ask great questions and listen. Remember, we were given two ears and one mouth for a reason.

C) Describe your solution. Describe what you and your product are able to do. Give an accurate time frame for delivery or completion of key items, and the results they can expect and look forward to. How long is it going to take for your prospect to go from new client to happy client? Now is the time to under-promise, so later you can over-deliver.

You don't need to include every feature of your product, just the ones that matter to them (which you will have discovered when you identified their problem or need). What has to happen between now and nirvana? What will you do? What will they need to do, if anything? And most importantly, how will their life be better as a result of saying "yes" to your offering?

D) Emphasize the benefits the prospect can expect from your products or services. Take the time to create a list of reasons purchasing your product or service makes sense. While explaining all the features and benefits to the client may seem like a good idea, really try to hit home with the ones the client mentioned in the needs analysis.

- It saves time, money, effort, and energy.
- It provides a solution.
- It goes faster.
- It makes you look and feel better.
- It's safe.

- It's healthy.
- It makes you smarter.
- It's fun and exciting.
- It will free up time for other things, like family and vacations.

People buy with emotion and justify with logic. You'll want to lead with stories and real life examples of how your product will solve the problems that are keeping them up at night, so they *feel* compelled to say "YES!" when you ask for the sale. You'll also want to provide lots of logical reasons for purchasing your product or service, because this step helps them to justify the excitement you've created so they feel good about their decision to buy from you.

These first components, A-D, can and should get the client excited! In order to do that, however, *you* must be excited, too. Enthusiasm is contagious, and if you don't have it, you can't share it. An unenthusiastic prospect does not buy!

Note: This is another place that your Life S.A.V.E.R.S. come in handy. A solid morning practice that includes visualizing and affirming your enthusiasm and puts you in a peak emotional state each morning will spill over into your interactions with prospects.

E) Present the price for your product or services, in a way that leaves your prospect with no other conclusion than, "Yes, I'll take it!" This may include presenting different options for different packages or add-on options. I recommend always sharing fees and prices at the end, rather than the beginning, when you've had a chance to differentiate your product and build so much value in your offering that the perceived value (in the mind of the prospect) significantly exceeds the price.

One of the most powerful keys to optimizing your prospect's perception of price is to leverage the *law of contrast.* The law of contrast states that when two items are presented, one after the other, the second item is always perceived in contrast with the first. This is why stores always put items on sale. From department stores to car lots, slashing prices is an effective way of creating contrast, in the mind of the prospect, between the original price and the sale price. For example, if you're shopping at the mall and find a shirt you *really* like for $85, your initial feeling might be, *wow, that's a lot of money*. If, upon further investigation you discover a 50% off sticker and realize you can get it for $42.50, you might think, *I don't want to miss out on these incredible savings*, and you buy the shirt!

Think about this for a second. Was it the actual price of $42.50 that prompted you to buy the shirt *now*, or was it the contrast between the original price and the sale price? Surely it was the contrast. It wasn't what you ended up paying that compelled you to buy; it was how much you were saving. To be more specific, it was the emotional response that the contrast created within you. This is the power of *the law of contrast*, and it's something that you'd be wise to leverage on every sales presentation you ever deliver.

You'll also need to help your prospect justify the investment with logical reasons, including statistics and hard facts if possible. When they are both emotionally compelled to buy your product and they can justify making the purchase, they'll make the purchase.

Your client's reaction to your price should let you know if you have built enough value in your product or service during your presentation. People make purchasing decisions not on price, but on what they are getting in return for that price.

F) Close the sale. Take a moment to remind your prospect why you and/or your company are the best choice. Make them feel at ease with their buying decision. Ask your closing question, and then stop talking and let them buy. In the next chapter, we will go in depth on how to make closing easier and more comfortable than it's ever been, for both you and your prospects.

G) Collect referrals. Remember: referrals are your *potential income*, and the more referrals you have to call, the more potential income that is available to you, just waiting for you to claim it. Learning how to generate an unlimited supply of referrals gives you unlimited potential for your income. Even for the most experienced salesperson, the following five battle-tested, proven strategies will give you a detailed road map to the land of what I like to call "referral bliss"—a place where you always have more prospects to call than you have time to call them! Sounds nice, doesn't it?

Here are five keys to beginning your journey to referral bliss:

1. **Memorize, practice, and deliver a consistent referral approach, every single time.** The number one key to developing an unlimited supply of referrals is to have a rock solid approach. This may seem obvious, but very few salespeople do this well. As a result, they're always *hunting* for new leads. Even top producers fall into the trap of *not* collecting referrals from every customer, largely due to not adhering to a precise approach, consistently, with every single prospect. As a result of inconsistency in your approach, your referral results will be inconsistent. If you are not 100 percent *confident* in getting referrals when you deliver your approach, your customers will not be 100 percent *comfortable* in referring you to their friends. You'll find yourself riding the *referral roller coaster*, at times running low or even running OUT of people to call. But when you memorize and stick to using the same word-for-word approach every time, you're able to master it, and deliver it with confidence and expectancy.

2. **Set a positive expectation for referrals in the beginning of your presentation.** The number two key to consistently collecting more referrals than you can handle is creating a positive expectation for your prospect to give them to you. If you don't plant a seed early on that you will be asking for referrals later in your presentation, not only are you setting yourself up for failure, but you are leaving it up to *your customer* to decide whether giving you leads is a good or a bad thing. Wouldn't it make more sense for you to take responsibility for creating a positive expectation about the act of giving referrals than to let your prospect decide, based on their non-existent experience of referring you? After all, you're the only one who *knows* how much their referrals are going to love meeting you! Right?

3. **Here's an example of what you can say to set up a positive expectation, in the beginning of your presentation** (and feel free to customize it to fit your style): "Bob, thank you so much for meeting with me, today. I really appreciate your time and promise I'll do my best to make sure you get significant value

from our time together. What I'm here to (show you/help you with/discuss/assess) is _____, but my goal is not to try and *sell* you anything. If you end up liking what I show you and think it's a good fit, of course we'll explore your options. But my primary goal is simply that you get so much value from today that you'd feel comfortable recommending me to anyone you think could benefit from my product—just like your colleague, Jim, recommended me to you. That's really my favorite part of what I do: just about every person I meet with is a referral of someone I've already met with, so that way it's a win-win for everyone. But like I said, I really want to focus on how you can get as much value from our time today as possible."

By planting the seed for referrals, early on, it becomes much more comfortable when you bring it up at the end of your presentation. At that point, you're really just reminding them of what you've already told them. Your prospect won't be caught off guard, and thus, will be much more likely to give you referrals.

4. **Ask for 10–15 referrals, and expect to get *at least 10*.** Now, the number of referrals you ask for is somewhat arbitrary, but the point is: *don't hope to get referrals; expect to get referrals.* Whether you ask for 10 or 50, your expectation (or lack thereof) is contagious. If your customer senses that you do not expect to *get* 10+ referrals from them, they will not be confident nor feel comfortable *giving* you 10+ referrals. Your results are born from your expectations, and you tend to get whatever you expect. Your confidence in asking for 10–15 referrals will increase the more you practice your approach, and even more so once you start to collect 10–15 referrals from each of your prospects.

5. **Let them see that you already get lots of referrals.** In the approach listed above, you leveraged the power of *social proof* when you reminded them that *they were referred* by a friend or colleague. Depending on what tool you use to collect referrals, you can take leveraging social proof to another level. Personally, I like to use an old fashioned notebook to collect

all of my referrals, when I'm sitting face-to-face with a prospect or customer. As I'm finishing up reciting my (memorized) referral approach, I flip through my notebook, letting my customers see pages with 15+ referrals already written on each. This allows them to see evidence that it is completely normal for people to give me 10 referrals, and it sets their expectancy and makes them feel comfortable doing the same, since people tend to feel comfortable doing what everyone else is doing. If you don't already have pages in your referral notebook with 10 names, ask your friends and family to fill up a few pages of 15 for you, so you have something to get you started.

6. **Expect to hear "no" and be ready for it.** Remember, the average sale is made the fifth time it's asked for. The same goes for referrals, so expect and be ready to handle an objection or two. Realize that objections are often given, *not* because they represent some deep virtue, value, or principle held by your customer, but because it simply takes less effort to give you an objection, like, "I don't do that to my friend" or "I don't know anyone" than to write down a list of referrals. Just be ready to reemphasize and remind them how important it is to you, how much you enjoy meeting your customers' friends and colleagues, and how much value *their* friends and colleagues will get from meeting you. After all, they will get value from meeting you, right?

Step 3: Practice

Include a significant amount of time to practice your presentation until it rolls off of your tongue like your long-memorized phone number. At some point, the words will become yours and they will sound conversational. Remember this: practice doesn't make perfect, but it does make *permanent*.

Step 4: Stand (or sit) and Deliver

Finally! It's time to give your presentation.

In many sales scenarios, this could be the first communication between you and your prospect, so a first impression is critical.

I know it doesn't take me long to decide if I like someone or not, and I bet it takes you about a nanosecond to size someone up. Be prepared—your prospects are making the same judgments from the moment they lay eyes on you.

It's up to you to maximize your chances of a great first impression by carrying yourself with confidence, having a smile on your face, and making good eye contact. In other words, be friendly, open, and have a fantastic attitude.

Selling is about relationships, and people like doing business with people they know, like, and trust. Throughout your presentation, take the time to find out about your prospect's interests, their family, what they do when they are not working. We are not just chatting about the weather here, we are focused and intentional in building a relationship by finding out what is important to the client and showing genuine interest. They have to trust the person who is making the sale, and that's *you*.

You must genuinely care for each person who is spending their valuable time to meet with you, and you need to convey that caring. Be in a state of curiosity. Find out what the person across from you is about, to the extent you can. The more you can connect with someone, the better the entire sales process is going to be.

Remember, it is not always what you say to the prospect, but *how you say it* that makes an impression. During your presentation, you must convey confidence, compassion, knowledge, expertise, flexibility, and concern. If you can do these well, you can often establish a strong bond with your prospect that will last through this sale and into future sales, and referrals.

For your sales delivery to be most effective, follow these important tips:

• Always speak in a confident tone of voice, at a good pace, and very deliberately. If you feel uneasy during any part of the presentation, it will show! If your self-confidence needs some work, don't worry; you are not alone. Everyone struggles with self-doubt. We all have a voice inside of us that questions whether or not we are good enough and have what it takes to succeed. To build your self-confidence, add statements to your list of affirmations, create a short mental visualization of you in your most confident state, and seek out specific books that address ways you can boost your self-confidence.

- Be sure that the prospect is following what you are saying. It's easy to assume the others also have the knowledge we take for granted. Check in by periodically asking if there are any questions. Use phrases such as, "Does that make sense?" to ensure your prospect is keeping pace with you.

- Keep your enthusiasm up to keep the prospect interested in what you are saying.

- If you are planning a demonstration as part of your presentation, design it step-by-step. When you think you have it down, do a few dry runs to make sure—don't learn on your prospect's time! It's no fun to have to apologize for a failed presentation. Better to fail on your own time, out of sight of your prospects.

Show and Tell

Used properly, visual aids can be tremendously effective. Research has shown that, despite varying learning modalities such as auditory and kinesthetic, all people are highly visual, and are more likely to be persuaded if visual aids are used. Even today, social media experts say that online content attracts more attention, gets more shares, and ultimately converts better when it uses images.

Remember, though, that presentation tools are just that: tools. They're supplements to a great presentation. I'm a big fan of keeping it simple, and visual aids can sometimes overpower your presentation and detract from your message. This is especially true if you're uncomfortable with them, or you find yourself explaining the audiovisual message. Presentation aids should enhance not detract from you and your message.

Sometimes, the most important visual aid is your product or service itself. If appropriate, you'll want to demonstrate what you offer. Remember, though, that most important visual aid is *you*. No slide deck is going to make up for a lack of preparation, or trump the value of your connection with your customer.

In addition to your being top-notch, here is a list of presentation aid options:

- **The product itself.** If you've got it to show off, by all means show it off.

- **Video.** Show your product in action or include the testimonial of an over-the-moon satisfied customer.

- **PowerPoint.** No video, no problem. Pull together some slides and personalize them to your customer and their company. Keep the presentation fast, factual, and fantastic.

- **In-office presentations.** Today you can use your tablet or iPad at the drop of a hat, regardless of location. So, if you can whip out your fancy device as part of your presentation, by all means, do it.

Step 5: The Post-Presentation Review

Whether you have closed the sale are not, you have an incredible opportunity to learn from every presentation. If your presentations are on-the-job training, think of reviewing your presentations after the fact as a skill accelerator.

Within a few hours, at most 24 hours, take some time (even five minutes) to jot down some notes in your journal about what went right, what you could do better next time, what you said that was effective, and what you want to change for your next opportunity.

The more presentations you do, the better you will get. Let's face it: the first time you give a presentation, you're nervous and concerned you'll forget key pieces and points. Don't worry. That's normal. Once you've said something a dozen times, you'll start to feel like it's second nature, and once you've given a presentation more than 100 times, you could give the presentation in your sleep! Every presentation you give builds your presentation-giving muscles. You get better and better with each one, and eventually you will be as good as, or better than, the guy down the hall who tops the sales charts month after month.

Being Authentic vs. Being Perfect

If all this seems like a lot of preparation for what might be as little as a few minutes with a prospect, think again.

All of the research, legwork, rough drafts, practice, reviewing, and more practice aren't just an effort to work harder than the next person. They're meant to drive your knowledge and your emotion about your offering so deeply and naturally into you that you're *no longer presenting.*

When you nail a presentation—when everything truly flows—I believe you reach a point where you've transcended the sales presentation as we think of it. You stop selling, stop pitching, stop hoping, or needing, and you reach a point of authenticity that is more powerful than any sales pitch.

We live in a time where people are craving connection and authenticity more than ever, and nowhere is this truer than in sales. The more a prospect can feel that you care about *them*—not just whether they buy—and that every word out of your mouth is sincere, the more connected they will feel to you and the less they will judge your presentation. The more authentic and honest you are, the more they'll look for ways to include you instead of rule you out.

You can't fake authenticity. But you can open yourself up to it, and prepare yourself to the greatest extent possible. If you're giving your presentation for the first time because it's literally your first day on the job, don't hide it. Bring the prospect in on your situation. Gaps in your product knowledge, having only a few months or years in business, or even lacking in key experience can sometimes be overcome with enthusiasm.

If you're a new salesperson, don't hesitate to let your prospect know. Tell them that you're new, so you're going to be deliberate because you want to do a great job with them. Your newness could be your secret weapon!

Let go of trying to be perfect, and instead, just be authentic. Be yourself. Simply be who you are. Love who you are, and others will too.

Does authenticity close a sale? It certainly goes a long way to doing so. But nailing your presentation isn't everything. It doesn't guarantee that your prospect will leap over the desk waving their Black American Express card, demanding a contract to sign.

You may have one more hurdle to clear ... and that's what our next chapter is for.

Your Sales Accelerator Steps

Step 1: Grab your journal. Write a list of the top five things you need to learn about your product and services and how it can help your clients. Write a list of the five things you should learn about each client before meeting with them.

Step 2: Schedule an hour to start researching your top three competitors and the key benefits and weaknesses of their product or service. Get to know your competition inside and out so that you know exactly what your competitive advantages are and you can effectively articulate those to your prospects. This step will also give you an even deeper understanding as to exactly who your Level 10 customers are and where to find them.

Step 3: Review and rehearse your current presentation. Does it meet the suggestions of this chapter? Find any places where your presentation could improve, and make those changes. Then, practice. Rehearse. Master your presentation.

Step 4: Each morning, during your *Miracle Morning*, take a minute to look over your appointments for the day. Then, one by one, visualize meeting with each prospect and assessing their needs. Picture everything going exactly as planned. You are getting great information from them that will really allow you to solve a problem for them. What questions are you asking? How are they responding? How much are you talking versus listening? By visualizing this first you will make executing it that much easier when face-to-face with your prospects.

TOP ONE PERCENT SALESPERSON INTERVIEW

Mike Huboky – Marketing Director, N2
Publishing

Mike Huboky bleeds passion and enthusiasm for the entrepreneurial spirit. He is a Hall of Fame inductee with Vector Marketing, where he spent 20 years developing his expertise in recruiting, sales, and leadership development. Mike has recruited and trained thousands of salespeople. Mike prides his success in sales on enthusiasm, passion, work ethic, and the ability to overcome adversity. Mike's attitude and mindset have propelled him to leadership positions in sales organizations, like his current position as Marketing Director at N2 Publishing.

Mike talks about the importance of building rapport in presentations with clients before promoting a product: "Once the wall is down, they are open to what I am pitching or talking about. Whether I am meeting with a CEO or an owner, I always see myself at their level."

"I build value in what I am selling and how it can impact *their* business. I ask questions along the way to make sure we are on the same page. Do you see how this can help your business grow? I ask a ton of questions that I know will get a *yes*. A sale is made up of lots of little yes's along the way."

"I try to make sure my customers know I have their best interest at heart. I keep in touch after the sale. Most salespeople are in and out and you never hear from them again."

What struck me most about Mike was his attitude and work ethic. Even when his presentation is at his best and he is closing his clients and helping them to purchase, he still focuses on the next client. "ACTIVITY, ACTIVITY, ACTIVITY is the key. Even if you're on the right track, you'll get run over if you don't keep moving."

MIRACLE MORNING SUCCESS STORY
Julie Thiry – Founder and Chief Yogi, 11Exhale

An avid practitioner of *The Miracle Morning*, Jeff Latham recommended the book to Julie, who downloaded it to read on her iPhone in December 2013. Now, almost a year and a half later, she is grateful for the impact the Life S.A.V.E.R.S. have had in her life.

"Before *The Miracle Morning* I lacked a clear direction and stability in my life. I felt as if I had a lot of activity but not the clarity or purpose that I now have thanks to *The Miracle Morning*. Before *The Miracle Morning* I felt as if I was just going through the motions of life every day but not in a centered way or a purpose."

Julie is experiencing great results with *The Miracle Morning*, because the "...process is a tool I use in order to set an intention for the day with a clear vision and clarity. By taking care of my mind in the morning, I am better able to focus on my business and family. Utilizing the Life S.A.V.E.R.S. formula has been my way of feeding myself first before I give to others. I have been able to spend less time working and more time pursuing my passion for yoga and time with family while still maintaining my workload within my business. The Miracle Morning has taught me to focus my energy to get more done."

With enthusiasm, she states: "I love having a powerful system that is only four percent of your day but has such an impact on everything within the day."

— 9 —

SALES ACCELERATION SKILL #3:

COMFORTABLE CLOSING

*"Selling is telling an emotionally compelling story
that inspires your prospects to see a new and bigger
possibility for themselves and then simply inviting
them to participate in that possibility with you/
your product or your service. When done elegantly
and artfully, your prospect is left better off after they
have met you than before."*

—KEVIN DONAHUE, Founder, Executive
Sales Source

For salespeople and prospects alike, closing is normally the most uncomfortable part of the sales process. This is largely because all human beings are afraid of making a *wrong* decision, so they would rather make no decision at all.

You've reached the point where you're ready to close the sale and are in need of a concrete "yes" or "no" response from your prospect. The tension is at its peak. Feeling nervous but eager, you look your prospect in the eye, and confidently ask for the order. Hoping to hear a resounding "YES!" you instead get an objection: *"I need to think about it."* Or *"I can't afford it."* Or worse *"I need to talk it over with my wife/business partner/ cat/ spirit guide/gardener...*

(or anyone else who isn't in the room and didn't see your incredible sales presentation!)"

But what if you could minimize or even remove that tension, so that closing became comfortable, easy, and even effortless? What if you were a master at handling objections *before* they came up, so that your prospects were always left with no option but to say, "YES!" and buy from you? What if, at the end of your presentation, you didn't even have to ask your prospect for the order, because your closing process was designed to comfortably lead them to a buying decision? If any of this sounds appealing, you're going to love this chapter.

Closing is a Conversation

Closing and handling objections shouldn't be reserved for the end of your presentation, but rather, think of closing as a conversation between you and a friend. If you were talking with your friend about buying a product that you personally own and love, and they gave you an objection or two, it wouldn't feel uncomfortable. You would just hear their objections, and handle them. Here's what that might look like:

"Hey Bob, you should totally get an iPhone. I love mine!"

[Objection] "Yeah, but I don't know if I need it. I just use my phone to make calls; don't think I would really use all of the features."

"I know what you mean; I thought the same thing. But it's so intuitive and easy to use that I'm able to do everything on it, no matter where I am. Even if I'm out of my office, I can answer all of my emails, text clients, update my calendar—which automatically syncs with my computer—and use the GPS to map my appointments. I don't have to lug my GPS with me anymore. It's literally like having a computer that does *everything*, in your pocket!"

[Objection] "But I travel so much, I'm afraid I would lose it or leave it on the plane."

"The fact that you travel is exactly why you should get it. I know you love movies. Did you know you can download movies and TV shows to watch on the plane?

"Really?! No, I didn't know that."

"Absolutely. And there are apps now for everything! You can track your expenses right on the phone. And get this; I can even take a picture of business cards and it automatically adds them to my database. In fact, the more we talk about it, the more I'm realizing that this could add so much value to your life and be a game changer for work.

[**Objection**] "But aren't those phones a lot more expensive? Business is kind of slow right now; I don't know if I can afford it. Maybe I should wait."

"If you mean more expensive than your flip phone, then yeah— the tank of gas I bought today cost more than your flip phone. But think about it, what other device do you have with you and use more often? Considering how much this can increase your productivity, it will pay for itself many times over. I would think of it as an investment in your business, plus it's a tax write-off. The sooner you get it, the sooner you can start streamlining a lot of your work processes to be more efficient, which will enable you to grow your business faster. I'll be happy to sit down with you and show you how to use it to improve your business so that the phone pays for itself in the first month or two. Seriously, the more we're talking about it, the more I'm realizing that this is a good investment for you. What do you think; why don't we go by the Apple store real quick and check it out?"

"All right. You sold me. Let's go."

Although Bob gave you three objections, you didn't take them as *rejections*. You just continued the conversation, comfortably, then addressed and handled his objections as they came up. It should be no different when you're meeting with a prospect.

What Objections Really Are

Let's start here: *An objection is not a "no."*

An objection is merely a concern. It is a request for more information. You may think that what you're hearing *feels* like a rejection and *sounds* like "no." But it isn't. You're hearing an objection, not a "no."

"I don't know if I can afford it," isn't *no.*

"I'm not sure if it's a fit for me," isn't *no.*

"I don't think I need it right now," isn't *no.*

What your prospect is really saying in each of these cases is, "I have a *concern.* I don't feel comfortable saying 'yes' *yet.* I need more information." Your job is to know the most common objections, like the back of your hand, expect to hear them from prospects, and be ready to respond gracefully and effectively to overcome them.

One of the biggest steps you can take to improve your closing ratio is to not allow your prospect's objections to discourage you from moving forward and closing the sale.

When you are truly engaged with your prospect, you're not rushing to quickly deal with their objections and move on to the close. You're trying to get to the heart of what they need to know in order to make the best buying decision. Listen to what they say, read their non-verbal signs, give them what they need, and you can turn any objector into a customer.

In my experience, every objection contains within it several questions. Your prospect might not phrase them as questions—they might not be statements with question marks at the end—but believe me, they are indeed questions. Your job is to a) understand what question is being asked and b) answer it. Because an objection isn't a "no." It's just a question—a request for more information and/or validation—in disguise.

Understanding that is the first step to becoming a master of handling objections and closing more sales than you ever have. It keeps you from taking an objection personally, getting defensive, or even combative with your prospect.

Beginning to Overcome Objections

When it comes to closing, the ability to overcome objections is a skill that is so intertwined that you will almost never find one without the other—kind of like salt and pepper. Master each of them and you will enjoy a multiplier effect in the form of more commissions in your pocket.

Whether the person in front of you buys from you or not, I hope you have connected with them on a deeper level, human being to human being, and you've shared your love of your product or service, along with some hard facts and figures, to bring them to a resounding, "Yes!"

But I have been, and still am, in the selling trenches with you, and I know that the no's can sometimes outnumber the yes's and sometimes by a wide margin.

No sooner have you mastered the art of the presentation and feel comfortable with it, then you'll experience prospect after prospect throwing up objections that are sometimes reasonable, and other times downright insane.

What's a salesperson to do? Don't worry; I've got you covered.

The toughest aspect of sales is often overcoming your prospect's objections. If even a single objection is not overcome, it can prevent your prospect from becoming a customer. You often don't know if objections are real or fabricated to cover up the real issue. For example, if a prospect doesn't feel they can afford your product, but they're embarrassed to tell you that, they might give you a completely random objection to avoid hurting their ego.

Speaking of ego, some prospects will object simply because they *can*. For some people, doing so feeds their ego, and they find it entertaining to torture their salespeople as much as possible. For the most part, though, if you treat each prospect with respect, even as they share reasons why they are hesitant to buy now, you will have a win-win for both of you more times than not.

But it doesn't matter how well prepared your presentation is, if you're not prepared to handle, overcome, and even *transcend* objections. I'm going to help you master the language to handle the five most common objections, and finally, how to close the sale. With the power of your Life S.A.V.E.R.S. added in for mental and emotional preparation, you'll see your closed sales numbers rising significantly and in a very short time.

As for how to master this crucial selling skill, it starts with understanding the five fundamental objections.

The Five Fundamental Objections

Attempting to rush your prospects through their decision-making process is going to lead to broken trust and well, no sale. Likewise, walking away empty-handed because you weren't prepared for objections is an opportunity wasted. The sweet spot is in the middle, in taking the time to respond sincerely and thoughtfully to the concerns your prospect has.

A sale *this close* to happening can fall apart because you don't take a deep breath, stop, and realize nearly all sales objections come down to one of five things:

1. Need
2. Want
3. Timing
4. Trust
5. Money

1. Need *(Do I need this?)*

At the most basic level, your prospect should have a need for what you're selling. Not just want it, but also *need* it. That need could be logical or emotional, or it could be both, but regardless, they have to decide they need what you offer.

Often prospects don't realize they have a problem or that they need what you're selling, until you meet with them and open their eyes to the need. For example, when Hal and I used to sell Cutco Cutlery, more than 90 percent of our prospects didn't know they needed new knives. It wasn't until we went over to their homes and had them cut various foods, comparing their knives' cutting ability with Cutco, that they realized how dull and ineffective their knives were. The need was already there, but they were blind to it until that moment. It's your job to help your prospects become aware of needs they may not have previously been aware of.

Some *need* questions that prospects typically ask themselves, include the following.

Will I use this?

Is this the best product or service for me?

Is this the best option compared to the competitor?

Will it work? Will it solve my problem?

Will I regret this?

How will this make me feel?

Remember, they may not verbalize these thoughts or frame them as questions. Your job is to answer all of them during your presentation before they come up. Do that, and you'll get a lot more yes's the first time you ask for the sale.

2. Want *(Do I want it?)*

Interestingly enough, *want* is often more important than *need* when it comes to selling. Even if your prospect needs your product, if they don't want it, they're not likely to buy it. Your job as a salesperson is to create an atmosphere and offer that are so enticing your prospect would be crazy not to want it! (Note: there are crazy prospects out there.)

How do you create such an atmosphere?

First, you address the *need* questions that we just covered. Establishing a need is the first step in enticing your customer to want what you're selling.

Second, you show up with a genuine belief and enthusiasm for what you're selling and the value/benefits that it will provide for your prospect. Enthusiasm is contagious! **Warning:** Don't be obnoxious. There is a fine line between being authentically excited about your product and trying to manufacture over-the-top enthusiasm. Your enthusiasm must be authentic, sincere, and genuine. Just be yourself—the enthusiastic version.

Third, you bring out *their* enthusiasm. To prime the pump, I like to ask my prospects what's new and exciting in their lives or businesses. Getting a prospect to talk about what they're excited about puts them into a heightened emotional state. Then, when you present your product while they are in that state, they will naturally be more excited about your product, simply because they're already feeling that way.

Fourth, find out what your prospect wants. Specifically, find out what they want that your product can give them. This is something that you'll be doing throughout your presentation through all of the needs assessing and fact-finding questions that you'll be asking. Once you know what they want (because they told you), then you repeat it back to them. "I know you said you want ice in your igloo, Mr. Eskimo, and our lifetime ice maker will give it to you."

3. Timing *(Do I need it now?)*

I recently bought a new car, and I absolutely love it. I needed a new car for a while, but the timing had to be perfect for me to buy, and until certain stars had aligned, I just wasn't ready.

There are, however, ways to shift timing. This can be done by creating urgency through temporary discounted pricing and other compelling benefits for purchasing within a specific time frame (i.e., *today*). In many cases, there's a financial advantage to prospects buying now as opposed to later. For example, if your product is going to save them money over the long run, then the sooner they buy from you the sooner they can start saving money and the more money they will save. A prospect with a financial issue may truly be able to buy now and simply not realize it.

An "I don't need it right now" objection may also mean your prospect does not actually know how beneficial having your product or service will be for them. Many people feel they can't use business coaching, for example, because they're too stressed and busy. But business coaches *lower* your stress levels and help to make you more effective and efficient. Sometimes, the very reason people think they "don't need it now" is the same reason they truly *do*. Once they understand that, they become open to the possibility of taking action now versus later or never.

Sometimes prospects really *are* planning for a purchase that will happen later. If your prospect truly needs what you're selling, but they don't need it *now*, it may mean you're going to have to step back and stay in touch until they are. Whether they're on a find-and-purchase today trip, or an information-gathering mission, you need to discover their situation so you can steer them down the right path.

Remember: while you can rarely control a person's timing, you can influence it by giving them compelling, logical reasons to buy now. You do this by pointing out why it's in their best interests to do so, *during your presentation*, and not waiting until they've voiced their objections.

4. Trust *(Do I trust you?)*

Trust comes down to whether or not the prospect believes you can do what you say you can do or if your product or service is truly going to deliver what they need. If they do believe, it mitigates risk and gets you closer to the sale.

Think about it: When you trust someone and feel like you have enough relationship with them, you are more likely to open up and share what is really going on in your mind. Prospects are no different, and when you have developed the right kind of trust and relationship with them, they will give you a peek behind their curtain. The information you find behind it can help you to help them at the highest level.

The higher the risk to the prospect in the sale—in commitment, cost, time, energy, and reputation—the more trust is required. *You need enough of a relationship with your prospect for them to trust you.* You build this trust the old fashioned way … You earn it.

A trustworthy salesperson is one who always looks out for the best interests of his or her prospects and customers and who will take a hit in their commissions, or even walk away without making a sale, if that's the right outcome for the customer. A trustworthy salesperson has impeccable integrity and always doesn't the right thing, even if it's not the easy thing for them to do.

How trustworthy are you? Do you *always* do what's in your customers' best interests, even if it doesn't produce the largest commissions for you?

To become a rock solid, high-trust salesperson, incorporate the benefits into your affirmations. Here are a few that you can add:

I am committed to being a high-trust salesperson and doing what's best for my prospects and customers because I want to build an impeccable reputation and a successful, long-term career (which is far more important than any individual sale).

To build a successful career, I will come from a place of service, always looking to add value and give more than I take.

I always do what's in the best interests of my prospects and customers, even if that means that I give up commission in the short term.

If you find yourself resisting any of these affirmations, that's normal. Most salespeople don't operate this way and have been conditioned to look out for themselves. Remember that affirmations are one of the most effective and efficient ways to reprogram your subconscious mind with the beliefs, principles, and behaviors that you need to take your success to the next level. Even if this mindset is foreign to you, or if you've struggled with this mindset in the past, now is the time to take your SELF to the next level so you can take your SALES to the next level.

5. Money *(Can I afford it?)*

Money is the last of the four objections for good reason: it's the least important.

Sound crazy? It's true. If someone needs what you have, and needs it now, and trusts you? They'll almost *always* find the money. The money becomes a detail to be sorted, not an objection to be countered.

The money objection is common, though. The trick is that sometimes it's real and sometimes it isn't. Your first job is to decide which.

Is your prospect asking the question, "Can I afford this?" or are they asking, "Do I *want* to afford this?"

Your prospects might be tire-kickers and genuinely have no budget for what you're offering (although once you've followed the steps in chapter 8 and shifted from *trying to sell to anyone* to staying focused on *attracting Level 10 customers*, this should be less of an issue). Or they may be using the money objection to score the best deal they can get. You'll need to become very skilled at crafting and delivering questions that will help you uncover where your prospect sits in terms of their budget.

For those whom money truly is the issue, make sure that you've clarified *all* aspects of the financial picture. Your prospect may not understand that you provide financing, for example, or realize that buying a particular product may be an expense up front, but actually save them more money over time. My favorite brand of computer, for example, is known for being significantly more expensive than the competitive products, but they last longer, are designed better, have less downtime, and lower maintenance costs. A higher up-front investment will save the purchaser time and money over the long term.

Concerns vs. Objections

There are essentially two ways you can handle objections: *after* your prospect has voiced them or *before* your prospect has said a word.

The best time to handle an objection is not after it's come up but rather to anticipate, address, and answer all of the common questions and concerns that your prospects are likely to have before they ever say them out loud.

While the terms "objection" and "concern" can be used interchangeably, consider this important distinction between a concern and an objection:

Concern: A common thought or question that *most* prospects have, which can be addressed or answered in advance so that they *feel* good making the *decision* to buy TODAY.

Objection: A decision that your customer has *already* made as to why they *cannot* buy from you today.

Think of an objection a bit like a brick wall that's already been established in the mind of the customer, and now you have to break through it. Armed with what you now know, you have the power to do that. However, a concern is more like a speed bump, which if you're expecting, you can gently roll over and leave it behind you. Concerns are to be anticipated and handled in advance before they become objections in the prospect's mind.

Preparing to Handle Concerns (In Advance)

Use your common sense, experience, and the experience of your colleagues to think through and make a list of all the common concerns that your prospects are likely to have. For starters, reference *The Five Fundamental Objections*. While *Need, Want, Timing, Trust,* and *Money* are a great place to start, each product has its own unique concerns and objections. For example, back when we sold Cutco Cutlery, we would often hear objections like, "I'm afraid of sharp knives" or "I don't need a *set* of knives; I use one knife for everything." Your product or service likely generates unique concerns for your prospects, which you can begin to anticipate and overcome, in advance.

Stop reading for a few minutes, and start making a list of as many common concerns and objections you can think of, and then schedule time, either now or later, to script your answers or counters to handle them during the course of your presentation. Take time to actually write down objections you have heard, or know of, and script out a logical and emotional counter for each one.

Success Note: Keep in mind that when you come up with what you're going to say during your presentation to address and handle common concerns in advance, you're also creating the basis of what you'll say when prospects bring their concerns up again, which they will. Just because you handle a concern in advance doesn't mean that it's not still weighing on your prospect's mind. But, it does mean that you've already handled it, and you simply have to remind them of what you've previously said. This is much more effective than passively waiting for the prospect to be the first to raise the objection.

Again, preparation is key. Practicing means you won't have to think on your feet during a stressful selling situation—you'll already have the answer on the tip of your tongue

Using Clarifying Questions

Just as your prospect has questions, so do *you*. In fact, questions are one of the greatest objection-tackling tools in your sales kit. You can use questions in two different ways in the closing process.

a) To Recognize Objections

First, you can use questions to tease out objections along the way. It's important that you take the time to develop the ability to recognize the real objections as early as possible in each sales conversation. This allows you to quickly understand, address, discuss, and ultimately overcome sales objections, closing more deals before you know it.

You can ask closing questions even when you're miles from the sale, such as:

- "How does that sound?"
- "Are you with me so far?"
- "Does that make sense?"
- "Would that be a good fit for you?"
- "Would that help you solve your problem?"

When I'm showing homes, I'm constantly asking, "What do you think?" "How does this look to you?" and "Is this what you had in mind?" And each time I'm paying close attention to what I'm hearing, including the tone, language, any hesitations, or even enthusiasm and what I'm seeing in my prospect's body language and facial expressions.

b) To Transcend Objections

Next, you can use questions that engage your clients on a different level, and cause them to think more deeply about their perceived objections. You will want to ask powerful clarifying questions, such as the following:

- "If you made the perfect purchase, what would that look like?"
- "Is there anything standing in the way of your purchasing now?"
- "What other information do you need in order to make an informed decision?"

Take time to jot down your own clarifying questions, and just like your presentation and handling of objections, spend the time to memorize them until they are second nature. Properly used, questions can bridge the gap between prospect and buyer.

Success note: when you come from a place of genuine curiosity, you will be able to ask clarifying questions and your prospects will readily answer them. When they feel like you are on their side and not asking because you're trying to wrap up the sale today, they'll open up and share what's really going in their particular situation. The only way to do that is to be authentic and to genuinely look for a win-win arrangement. If you can't find one, you will gain more by telling someone when you do not think it is the right fit for them. It may even allow for you to create new business opportunities by asking for referrals because they will respect the fact that you had their best interests at heart.

And Finally, It's Time for the Close

At some point, you'll have heard every objection and either your prospect will take out their checkbook or you'll need to help them cross the finish line. It's time for your prospect to buy now, decide to wait until later, or elect to go a different direction entirely.

Your ability at this point to ask for the sale is absolutely essential to your success. Up until now, you've laid the groundwork for the sale by qualifying your prospects, prospecting to find the right prospects, making an awesome presentation, developing a solid, comfortable relationship, all while addressing concerns and optimizing objections. If you can keep in mind that even if 80 percent of the people you talk to aren't going to buy (which is true by some statistics), you can go for the close knowing you've done everything you can do, with integrity, to help your prospect make the best buying decision for them.

While some sales experts will preach ruthless closing tactics, that's not part of *The Miracle Morning for Salespeople* philosophy. If you've done your job and presented what you're selling effectively, getting to a successful close won't require any sneaky or under-handed techniques.

There are four methods that I recommend for closing the sale, and you can decide which of these feels the most comfortable for you. Or, you can try all four to figure out which method you like best. As your presentation is nearing the end, before you transition into the close, start by asking your prospect, "Do you have any questions or concerns that I haven't covered so far?"

If the prospect says, "No," you can then lean forward and confidently transition into one of these four closing methods. If they ask more questions, they are still interested. If they're asking, keep answering.

Method 1: The Comfortable Close

The first way to ask for the buying decision is the most simple of all. You can say some variation of "So, what do you think?"

This is a disarmingly effective closing technique because it doesn't force a prospect into the uncomfortable position of having to give you a definitive yes or no answer. If they still have unre-solved concerns (some of which they may not have shared with you yet), and you ask if they *want to buy*, you're setting yourself up to hear a "No."

Instead, by delivering a great presentation and simply asking "So, what do you think?" you create a comfortable opportunity for your prospect to share what's on their mind. If they're ready to buy, then that's what they're thinking, and they'll answer with some variation of "I think this sounds great! Do you take Visa?"

On the other hand, if they still have concerns, you've created a safe space for them to share their concerns, and then the two of you can simply continue the comfortable closing conversation. Handle each concern, and then move on to my second favorite comfortable closing question: "How does that sound?" You'll either get "That sounds great. I'll take it!" or they'll share more concerns. Either way, you simply continue the conversation until all of their concerns have been addressed and handled.

Success Note: When you say to your prospect "So, what do you think?" your voice should be upbeat and confident. Your tone should trail up toward the end of the sentence and communicate positive expectation as you ask the question. In fact, this holds true for all four of these methods.

Method 2: Give it a Try

The second method to ask for the buying decision is to say some variation of "Why don't you give it a try?"

Our nature is to answer questions, and when you ask this one, people automatically ask themselves, *Why DON'T I give it a try?*

Or you can say "Why don't you give us a try?" Or you can even say "Are you ready to take it?" or "It seems like this is the perfect time for you to move forward, don't you agree?"

You then reinforce this by adding the words "And I'll take care of all the details." Often a prospect doesn't know how much they wanted to buy until you offered to take care of all the details.

Method 3: Assume the Sale

The second method you can use is to proceed as if you just got a *yes*. You use these words: "The next step (in the process) is this." Then go on and describe the plan of action (such as: I will send/give you my contract) and wrap up the sale just as if the person had said, "I'll take it!"

This is truly my favorite. Personally, I believe this close is the easiest and most comfortable for many of my clients because it almost makes the decision for them. People have trouble taking the leap. Because I have typically closed them with small closes throughout the process, I assume they already want to move forward with me or they wouldn't still be sitting here at the end. If they have questions, they will still ask, and I will happily answer to make sure they feel comfortable moving forward, but most of the time, clients just sign at this point.

You will know instinctively if assuming the sale is the right thing to do. This is one of the most popular closing methods used by the highest paid salespeople in every industry.

Again, be sure to add, "And I'll take care of all the details."

Method 4: Ask for Authorization

My final suggestion for an effective closing method is to ask for their authorization. At the end of the sales conversation, you hand your order form or contract to your prospect and say "If you'll sign here and authorize this, we can get started." A prospect ready to buy will sign it, and most likely *they will be smiling*. If they aren't ready, they will throw up more objections, and you'll have more questions to answer.

There's one more scenario that may occur: your prospect stops talking altogether. They might be going over the facts and figures in their head. They might be trying to figure out how to pay for it, get financing, or contemplating where they could borrow the money.

If a prospect goes silent, ask them if they'd like a few moments to contemplate the situation. Give them the space and time they need.

Asking for the Order

If you don't ask, you can't get. You won't get the sale, the prospect won't get what they came to buy, and nobody wins.

That's why successful salespeople courageously *ask for the order.*

If you're hesitant to ask for the sale, I completely understand. Especially in the beginning, it can be uncomfortable to ask for the order. That's normal. Asking for anything, and getting more comfortable with it over time, is like building a muscle in the gym. The first time your trainer hands you 35-pound dumbbells, you might look at him like he's crazy! But eventually, those same dumbbells will be your warm-up weight. The more you ask, the more comfortable you'll feel asking. Practice doesn't only make perfect, it makes progress.

If you're still hesitating when it's time to ask, think about this: wouldn't you rather know where someone stands? The only true way to know is to ask. If they say "No, and by the way, you're ugly," then you can be offended. Otherwise, you're just collecting information and can move forward in the way that works best for both you and for the prospect. Look at it this way: if you ask, and you get a solid "no" (or a "not right now"), then you can move on to the next prospect without wasting more of your time.

When you've done everything right and you're sitting with your Level 10 prospect, you have an obligation to serve them. If they haven't gotten up to leave, and if they are still interacting with you, they are still interested. Ask for the order!

Congratulations, if you're not already the top salesperson in your office, territory or company, you absolutely can be! Nothing can stop you! Well, except for *the old you*, but through daily affirmations and visualization you'll be immediately upgrading your thoughts and beliefs to reflect *the new and improved you*.

I have one more strategy up my sleeve. When you're ready for the next level of selling, turn the page...

Your Sales Accelerator Steps

Step One: In your journal, write your list of the 10 most common objections that you have either heard from your clients in the past or expect to hear from them in the future. Look for spots in your presentation where you can address common *concerns* early on, before they're voiced as objections. Remember, the best time to answer an objection is before it ever comes up. Script out what you will say during your presentation and schedule time to memorize and practice so that handling concerns and objections becomes second nature for you.

Step Two: Decide which of the four closing methods you want to try first, and practice it.

Step Three: Before every meeting with a client, take a few minutes to visualize yourself closing the sale and gaining a new customer. See yourself delivering a flawless presentation, including a comfortable closing conversation. See objections coming up, and you handling them with ease. Notice how you answer them. Then assume the sale, and close the deal.

TOP ONE PERCENT SALESPERSON INTERVIEW

Mitchell Ackerman – National Account
Manager, Canon Business Process Services, Inc.

Mitchell's trip to the top one percent involved several twists and turns, including several restaurants, a few years in real estate development, and now landing in business-to-business services sales. Even with all the shifts and turbulence, Mitchell has experienced a tremendous level of success along the way. Mitchell prides himself on his consistent success through management and ownership changes and major product cycle shifts. More importantly, he accomplished it all without sacrificing his family, his friends, or himself.

"I was pretty much successful from the start, winning rookie of the year honors my first year and finishing in the top in my category for the first six years. Despite the apparent immediate success, there was a learning process that involved learning about selling internally and externally, negotiating with procurement organizations, and how to change with shifting markets and technologies. Learning what not to sell and how to defend that stance. There is always learning going on if you want to remain on top."

Mitchell had some interesting thoughts on closing to share because he rarely has to close at the end of a presentation. "Truthfully, I rarely have to close the sales. Clients are normally asking me how to move it forward. However, when I do, I normally use timelines to force decisions or scarcity of resources if we don't implement by a certain point in time. In the business I usually choose to pursue, I know if it's not a fit early enough in the post-proposal sales cycle to know if a close is even possible."

So how do we avoid this awkward pause at the end where we have to close: "Listening will solve many more problems and close many more sales than talking. The key to sales is learning what people already want to buy or do and selling it to them. Your role as a salesperson is to extract the buyer's preferences and then mold your company's product or service to deliver on those preferences."

MIRACLE MORNING SUCCESS STORY
John Israel – Hall of Fame Sales Representative,
Cutco Cutlery

After meeting Hal Elrod at a conference, John decided to read *The Miracle Morning*. He was resistant at first, because he (like a lot of us) was not a "morning person."

Experiencing hit-and-miss results was due to his "inconsistent consistency." He said, "Before I read *The Miracle Morning* I used to be consistently inconsistent. I'd get motivated, work my tail off, burn out, overindulge, relax, re-motivate myself, get back to work, etc., etc…

"*The Miracle Morning* is my way of doing those things I know to do that put me in a peak energy and performance state. Having routine and consistency is the only thing I've found to get consistent results instead of repeating that cycle."

"Three areas that have made the greatest difference in my personal and professional life are: waking up early, reading, and writing. "Waking up early is the only way I've found time to get done those things that are important that I always put off. It's 'John Time' between 6:00 AM and 8:00 AM"

He continued, "Every day I read between five and twenty pages. I've noticed reading really challenges my thinking and inspires me with actionable tips to help the areas I struggle with. There is too much information out there on any topic to be mediocre at anything. Writing has helped me tremendously to put my thoughts to paper that I can share with the world on Facebook or save for a book I'm writing. It accesses this creative part of my brain that is now ready for the day, and it gives me the opportunity to explore my thoughts and beliefs that anchor my convictions and reignites my self-confidence for the day. BOOM! *Miracle Morning*, baby!"

THE MIRACLE EQUATION

"For those who are willing to make an effort, great miracles and wonderful treasures are in store."
—ISAAC BASHEVIS Singer, Nobel Prize Winner (1978)

You might say that I've saved the best for last. It's time to take everything you've learned so far and bring it together with the ultimate success equation that ALL top achievers—in every field—use to consistently produce extraordinary results.

You know now that you can wake up early, maintain extraordinary levels of energy, direct your focus, and master the not-so-obvious selling skills. But I know you didn't read this far to just take your sales up a notch. You want to make quantum leaps and generate extraordinary results, right? Right. If you also apply what follows to your selling career, you're going to go much further: you're going to join the elite performers—*the top one percent.*

In order to make those leaps, there is one more crucial strategy that you must add to your sales toolbox, and it's called The Miracle Equation.

The Miracle Equation is the underlying strategy that Hal used to consistently break sales records, become one of the youngest individuals ever inducted into his company's hall of fame, and go on to become a number one bestselling author and international keynote speaker. But it's more than that. It is precisely the same equation that ALL top performers—that top one percent—have used to create awe-inspiring results, while the other 99 percent wonder how they do it.

The Miracle Equation was born during one of Hal Elrod's Cutco "Push Periods," a 14-day time period during which the company fostered friendly competition and created incentives to bring in record sales, both for the salesperson and the office.

This particular Push Period was special for two reasons. First, Hal was trying to become the first sales representative in his company's history to take the numer one spot for three consecutive Push Periods. Second, he'd have to do it while only being able to work for 10 of the 14 days.

Hal knew he needed to dig deep to achieve such a feat and that fear and self-doubt were a much greater hurdle than usual. In fact, he considered lowering his sales goal, based on the circumstances. Then he remembered what one of his mentors, Dan Casetta, had taught him: **The purpose of a goal isn't to hit the goal. The real purpose is to develop yourself into the type of person who can achieve your goals, regardless of whether you hit that particular one or not. It is who you become by giving it everything you have until the last moment—regardless of your results—that matters most.**

Hal made a decision to stick with his original goal, even though the possibility of failing to achieve it was a real risk based on the limited time frame. With only ten days to set a record, he knew he needed to be especially focused, faithful, and intentional. It was an ambitious feat, no question, and as you'll see, one that required him to really find out what he was made of!

Two Decisions

As with any great challenge, there are decisions that need to be made. Hal reverse-engineered the Push Period, by asking himself,

"If I were to break the record in just ten days, what decisions would I have to make and commit to in advance?"

Hal identified the two that would make the biggest impact. Only later did he realize that these were *the same two decisions that all top-performers make at some point in their careers.*

Those two decisions became the basis for The Miracle Equation.

The First Decision: Unwavering Faith

Knowing that he was already facing fear and self-doubt, Hal realized that in order to achieve the seemingly impossible, he would have to make the decision to maintain **unwavering faith** each and every day, *regardless of his results.* He knew that there would be moments when he would doubt himself and times when he would be so far off track that the goal would no longer seem achievable. But it would be those moments when he would have to override self-doubt with faith that was unshakeable.

To keep that level of unwavering faith in those challenging moments, Hal repeated what he calls his **"Miracle Mantra"**:

I will _____ (make the next sale, call 20 prospects, reach my goal), no matter what. There is no other option.

Understand that maintaining unwavering faith isn't *normal.* It's not what most people do. When it doesn't look like the desired result is likely, average performers give up the faith that it's possible. When the game is on the line, a team is down on the scorecards and there are only seconds left, it is only the elite performers—the Michael Jordans of the world—who, without hesitation, tell their team: *Give me the ball.*

The rest of the team breathes a sigh of relief because of their fear of missing the game-winning shot, while Michael Jordan made a **decision** at some point in his life that he would maintain unwavering faith, despite the fact that he might miss. (And although Michael Jordan missed 26 game-winning shots in his career, his faith that he would make every single one never wavered.)

That's the first decision that the world's elite make, and it's yours for the making, too.

When you're working toward a goal and you're not on track, what is the first thing that goes out the window? *The faith that the outcome you want so much is possible.* Your self-talk becomes *I'm not on track. It doesn't look like I'm going to reach my goal.* And with each passing moment, your faith decreases.

You don't have to settle for that. You have the ability and the choice to maintain that same unwavering faith, no matter what, and regardless of the results. You may sometimes doubt yourself or have a bad day, but you must find—and re-find—your faith that all things are possible and hold it throughout your journey, whether it is a ten-day push period, or a thirty-year career.

Elite athletes maintain unwavering faith they can make every shot they take. That faith—and the faith you need to develop—isn't based on probability. It draws from a whole different place. Most salespeople operate based on what is known as the *law of averages*. But what we're talking about here is the **law of miracles**. When you miss shot after shot—in your case, sale after sale—you have to tell yourself what Michael Jordan tells himself, "I've missed three, but I want the ball next, and I'm going to make that next shot."

And if you miss that one, *your faith doesn't waiver.* You repeat the Miracle Mantra to yourself:

I will _____ (make the next sale, call 20 prospects, reach my goal), no matter what. There is no other option.

Then, you simply uphold your integrity and do what it is that you say to yourself you are going to do.

An elite athlete may be having the worst game ever, where it seems like in the first three-quarters of the game, they can't make a shot to save their life. Yet in the fourth quarter, right when the team needs them, they start making those shots. They always want the ball; they always have belief and faith in themselves. In the fourth quarter, they score three times as many shots as they've made in the first three-quarters of the game.

Why? They have conditioned themselves to have unwavering faith in their talents, skills, and abilities, regardless of what it says on the scoreboard or their stats sheet.

And…

They combine their unwavering faith with part two of The Miracle Equation: **extraordinary effort.**

The Second Decision: Extraordinary Effort

When you allow your faith to go out the window, effort almost always follows right behind it. *After all,* you tell yourself, *what's the point in even trying to make the sale or achieve your goal if it's not possible?* Suddenly, you find yourself wondering how you're ever going to make the next sale, let alone reach the big goal you've been working toward.

I've been there many times, feeling deflated, thinking, *what's the point of even trying?* As a sales representative, if you're halfway through a competition and you should be at $50,000 and you're only at $7,500, you begin to think, "There's no way I can make it."

That's where extraordinary effort comes into play. You need to stay focused on your original goal—you need to connect to the vision you had for it, that big *why* you had in your heart and mind when you set the goal in the first place.

Like Hal, you need to reverse engineer the goal. Ask yourself *If I'm at the end of this time period, and this goal were to have happened, what would I have done? What would I have needed to do?*

Whatever the answer, you will need to take massive action and give it everything you have, regardless of your results. You have to believe you can still ring the bell of success at the end. You have to maintain unwavering faith and extraordinary effort—until the buzzer sounds. That's the only way that you create an opportunity for the miracle to happen.

If you do what the average person does—what our built-in human nature tells us to do—you'll be just like every other average salesperson. Don't! Remember: your thoughts and actions become a self-fulfilling prophecy.

Allow me to introduce you to your "edge"—the strategy, that when you use it, will skyrocket your goals, and practically ensure every one of your ambitions is realized:

The Miracle Equation

Unwavering Faith + Extraordinary Effort = Miracles

It's easier than you think. The secret to maintaining unwavering faith is to recognize that it's a mindset and a *strategy*—it's not concrete. In fact, it's elusive. You can never make *every* sale. No athlete makes *every* shot. So, you have to program yourself to automatically have the **unwavering faith** to drive you to keep putting forth the **extraordinary effort**.

Remember, the key to putting this equation into practice, to maintaining unwavering faith in the midst of self-doubt, is the Miracle Mantra:

I will _____, no matter what. There is no other option.

For me recently, it was "My sales team will close 50 transactions in a year without my daily presence, no matter what. There is no other option."

I manage an office of real estate agents, so my two main jobs are to provide coaching and training, as well as to continually find talented agents to join our office. I also have continued to build my sales team in another office approximately 45 minutes away. Managing an office and running a successful sales team is no small feat. When I accepted the team leader role last November, I knew I would need to create some counterbalance to keep my team growing and hitting our sales goals while effectively leading an office.

Sales definitely lagged in the first quarter—with a new job and one of the harshest winters Boston has seen in years, there would have been plenty of people who may have folded their team. Through persistence and vision, and having talented agents, the team has closed their first three deals, we will have several new listings as of the printing of this book, and we are actively writing offers with seven buyers. Never for a second have I doubted that my team would succeed. The slower start only increased my passion and intensity to achieve our goal through extraordinary energy and massive action, and it is paying off once again.

Once you set a goal, put that goal into the Miracle Mantra format. Yes, you're going to say your affirmations every morning (and maybe evenings, too). But all day, every day, you're going to repeat your Miracle Mantra to yourself. As you're driving or taking the train to the office, while you're on the treadmill, in the shower, in line at the grocery story, driving to pick up a prospect—in other words: *everywhere you go.*

Your Miracle Mantra will fortify your faith and be the self-talk you need to make just one more call or talk to one more person as they come through the door.

Bonus Lesson

Remember what Hal learned from his mentor, Dan Casetta: ***The purpose of a goal isn't to hit the goal. The real purpose is to develop yourself into the type of person who can achieve your goals, regardless of whether you hit that particular one or not. It is who you become, by giving it everything you have until the last moment—regardless of your results—that matters most.***

You have to become the type of person who *can* achieve the goal. You won't always reach the goal, but you can become someone who maintains unwavering faith and puts forth extraordinary effort, regardless of your results. That's how you become the type of person you need to become in order to consistently achieve extraordinary goals.

And while reaching the goal almost doesn't matter (almost!), more often than not, you'll reach your goal. Do the elite athletes win every time? No. But they win most of the time. And you'll win most of the time, too.

At the end of the day, you can wake up earlier, do the Life S.A.V.E.R.S. with passion and excitement, get organized, focused and intentional, and master every sales technique like a champ. And yet, if you don't combine unwavering faith with extraordinary effort, you won't reach the levels of sales success you're seeking.

The Miracle Equation gives you access to forces outside of any-one's understanding, using an energy that I might call God, the Universe, the Law of Attraction, even good luck. I don't know how it works; I just know that it works.

You've read this far—you clearly want success more than al-most anything. Commit to follow through with every aspect of selling, including The Miracle Equation. You deserve it, and I want you to have it!

Putting It into Action:

1. Write out the Miracle Equation and put it where you will see it every day: **Unwavering Faith + Extraordinary Effort = Mira-cles (UF + EE = M∞)**

2. What's your #1 goal for this year? What goal, if you were to accomplish it, would take your success to a whole new level?

3. Write your Miracle Mantra: *I will _____ (insert your goals and daily actions, here), no matter what. There is no other option.*

It is more about who you become in the process. You'll expand your self-confidence and, regardless of your results, the very next time you attempt to reach a goal, and every time after that, you'll be the type of person who gives it all they've got.

Closing Remarks

Congratulations! You have done what only a small percentage of people do: read an entire book. If you've come this far, that tells me something about you: you have a thirst for more. You want to become more, do more, contribute more, and earn more.

Right now, you have the unprecedented opportunity to infuse the Life S.A.V.E.R.S. into your daily life and business, upgrade your daily routine, and ultimately upgrade your *life* to a first class experience beyond your wildest dreams. Before you know it, you will be reaping the astronomical benefits of the habits that top achievers use daily.

Five years from now, your life, business, relationships, and in-come will be a direct result of one thing: *who you become.* It's up to you to wake up each day and dedicate time to becoming the best version of yourself. Seize this moment in time, define a vision for your future, and use what you've learned in this book to turn your vision into your reality.

Imagine a time just a few years from now when you come across the journal you started after completing this book. In it, you find the goals you wrote down for yourself—dreams you didn't even dare speak out loud at the time. And as you look around, you realize *your dreams now represent the life you are living*.

Right now, you stand at the foot of a mountain you can easily and effortlessly climb. All you need to do is continue waking up each day for your *Miracle Morning*, and use the Life S.A.V.E.R.S. day after day, month after month, year after year, as you continue to take your *self*, your *sales*, and your *success* to levels beyond what you've ever experienced before.

Combine your *Miracle Morning* with a commitment to master your sales acceleration skills, and use The Miracle Equation to create results that most people only dream of.

This book was written as an expression of what I know will work for you, to take every area of your life to the next level, faster than you may currently believe is possible. Miraculous salespeople weren't born that way—they simply dedicated themselves to developing themselves and their skills to achieve everything they've ever wanted.

You can become one of them, I promise.

Taking Action: The 30-Day Miracle Morning Challenge

Now it is time to join the tens of thousands of people who have transformed their lives, incomes, and sales careers with *The Miracle Morning*. Join the community online at **TMMBook.com** and download the toolkit to get you started *today*.

TOP ONE PERCENT SALESPERSON INTERVIEW
Andrea Waltz – Co-Owner, Courage Crafters
Inc.

Who better to talk about unwavering faith and extraordinary effort than the co-author of one of the best-selling sales books of all time, *Go For No! Yes is the Destination, No is How You Get There?* Andrea started with 10 years in retail sales before she and her husband, Richard, started a speaking and sales training company. Now, with over 20 years in the business, Andrea shares how her personal philosophies have contributed to their sales success.

"For us, it's been a mindset of this: For as long as it takes. At one point we had a sign on our wall that said Sell 1,000,000 copies of *Go For No* by XYZ date. And when that date came and went, and we had not accomplished it, we realized that the 1 million mark was the key. So we now have an 'as long as it takes' mindset. We will get there. Now, that's not to say you should not have timed goals, otherwise you might never get anything done! But for us, and for our mindset, it's a result that we will see happen no matter how long it takes us to reach it. So our #1 tip is to take your ultimate goal, your passion, and understand it may take longer than you wanted or expected. So, adopt the as-long-as-it-takes mindset if reaching that goal is truly what you want to have happen.

"My beliefs about being successful have a lot to do with how you define success in the first place. Let me start by saying, the enemy to success is the fear of failure. One of the things I have learned in my own business in the last 15 years is that, in order to see what works and what succeeds, you are going to try a bunch of stuff that will fail along the path. Learn, tweak, and try again as soon as you can.

"Re-craft and recreate an empowering definition of failure. Make failing a part of what you do on a weekly basis. When you start to see failure (getting rejected/a no) from a client/customer or from a big project you wanted as part of the process, your world can change. Your confidence can actually increase because you no longer measure yourself against results (did you get a "yes?"). You start measuring yourself by how gutsy you were, how many chances you took, and how much you failed. And then the success will be there for you when you do that enough."

MIRACLE EQUATION SUCCESS STORY
Robert Arauco – Marketing Director, Exuro
Marketing Concepts

At 19 years old, I was an up and coming sales rep for Vector Marketing, when I hired Hal Elrod to be my coach. He was one of the most successful salespeople in the history of our company, and I was hungry to take my success to the next level. My first goal: Do what few sales reps had ever done—and more than *double* what I had ever done—by selling over $20,000 of my product in a two-week "push period" (sales contest).

I was a little bit taken back when Hal didn't teach me any high level closing techniques, or how to go after whales, but instead he shared what he called the *Miracle Equation*, and described how it had worked for him. The strategy seemed a little "mystical" for my liking. But, Hal was the man. He had had multiple $20,000+ push periods, so I committed to maintain **unwavering faith** and give **extraordinary effort** everyday, *until the last possible moment.*

My first week I sold just over $10,000 and was on track to reach my goal! Then I ambitiously asked Hal, "Since the Miracle Equation has enabled you and the other sales reps that you coach to sell $20,000 in two weeks, do you think it could work for me to sell $30,000 in two weeks?"

"Well, Robert, my biggest push period is $27k, but I don't think there are any limits to the size of the miracle you can create! Plus, the purpose of your goal is to become the person you need to achieve such goals, so why not develop yourself into the type of person who *can* sell $30,000 in two weeks!"

So, I went for it. **Unwavering Faith + Extraordinary Effort** every single day, no matter what. I had some bad days. But I remained committed. When I concluded my last appointment, I was just over $25,000—about $5,000 short of my goal. So, I called Hal.

"I can't squeeze in any more appointments, but I do have a one-hour bus ride to the conference right now. What do you think I should do?"

"Robert, you've seen what happens when you maintain un-wavering faith and extraordinary effort, but there's still one more part—*until the last possible moment.* If I were you, during your bus ride tomorrow I would call every single person you did an appointment for—those who bought, and those who didn't. Thank them sincerely for their time and support, let them know how close you are to your goal, and that you're offering a one-time 50% discount if they'd like to add anything to their order. Be sure to emphasize how much you appreciate their time and/or the order they already placed, and that you don't expect them to get anything, but since you've never offered 50% off before, you wanted to at least extend the offer."

Although this strategy was completely out of my comfort zone, I was committed! I hung up with Hal, and began calling the 51 prospects and customers that I had seen during the past two weeks. Not only was everyone I spoke with happy to hear from me, four of them placed orders for a total of $5,100! I immediately called Hal…

"The Miracle Equation works! I hit $30,000 for push period!"

I have since applied The Miracle Equation to all of my person-al and professional goals, and have seen it generate extraordinary, *miraculous* results, time and time again.

A Special Invitation from Hal

Fans and readers of *The Miracle Morning* make up an extraordinary community of like-minded individuals who wake up each day, dedicated to fulfilling the unlimited potential that is within all of us. As creator of *The Miracle Morning*, it was my responsibility to create an online space where readers and fans could go to connect, get encouragement, share best practices, support one another, discuss the book, post videos, find an accountability partner, and even swap smoothie recipes and exercise routines.

I honestly had no idea that **The Miracle Morning Community** would become one of the most inspiring, engaged, and supportive online communities in the world, but it has. I'm blown away by the caliber of our 16,000+ members, which consists of people from all around the globe, and is growing daily.

Just go to **www.MyTMMCommunity.com** and request to join The Miracle Morning Community (on Facebook). Here you'll be able to connect with like-minded individuals who are already practicing *The Miracle Morning*—many of whom have been doing it for years—to get additional support and accelerate your success.

I'll be moderating the Community and checking in regularly. I look forward to seeing you there!

If you'd like to connect with me personally on social media, follow **@HalElrod** on Twitter and **Facebook.com/YoPalHal** on Facebook. Please feel free to send me a direct message, leave a comment, or ask me a question. I do my best to answer every single one, so let's connect soon!

THANK YOU TO ALL OF OUR *TOP ONE PERCENT* SALESPERSON INTERVIEWEES

Adrian Ivasic – Area Director/Owner Operator of Belle Meade Living at N2 Publishing

Andrea Waltz – Co-founder, Courage Crafters Inc. and bestselling author, *Go For No!*

Bob Urichuck – CEO, Velocity Sales Training, LLC and bestselling author, *Velocity Selling*

Corey Ackerman – Senior Partner, Cornerstone Search Company, LLC

Henry Evans – President, Time Zone Marketing and author, *The Hour A Day Entreprenuer*

Jerry Micozzi – Senior Clinical Business Manager, Cubist Pharmaceuticals

Jessica Halvorson – Consultant, Clever Container

Jim Bellacera – Founder, Successful Thinkers Network Inc.

Jim Kelley – Mortgage Originator, Mountain One Bank

John Ruhlin – Founder, The Ruhlin Group

Josh Mueller – Hall of Fames Sales Rep, Cutco Cutlery

Matt Gagalis – Vice President of Business Development, RxAnte

Mariana Pryhuber – Consultant, Paperly

Michael J Maher – Global Real Estate Consultant, REFERCO and bestselling author, *7L: The Seven Levels of Communication: Go From Relationships to Referrals*

Mike Huboky – Area Sales Director, N2 Publishing

Mitchell Ackerman – Enterprise Account Dir., Canon Business Process Services, Inc.

Pat Petrini – Owner of P&E Properties, LLC and Top Distributer for Modére

Rob Plannette – Branch Manager, Bath Fitter

Ruth Sinawi – #1 salesperson, Art Van Furniture

Sean McCullough – Founder/CEO, Young Eagle Entrepreneurs

Stacey Alcorn – Author of *REACH!*, serial entrepreneur and owner of RE/MAX Prestige, All American Title, P3 Coaching, and MyLittleBlackBox.com

Tom Cain – Realtor, RE/MAX CHOICE

ABOUT THE AUTHORS

HAL ELROD is the #1 best-selling author of what is now being widely regarded as "one of the most life-changing books ever written" (with over 800 five-star reviews on Amazon), *The Miracle Morning: The Not-So-Obvious Secret Guaranteed To Transform Your Life… (Before 8AM)*. Hal died at age 20. Hit head-on by a drunk driver at 70 miles per hour, he broke 11 bones, was clinically dead for six minutes, spent six days in a coma, and was told he would never walk again. Defying the logic of doctors and the temptations to be a victim, Hal went on to not only walk but to run a 52 mile ultra-marathon, become a hall of fame business achiever, an international keynote speaker, host of one of the top success podcasts on iTunes, called *Achieve Your Goals with Hal Elrod*, and most importantly… he is grateful to be alive and living the life of his dreams with his wife, Ursula, and their two children, Sophie and Halsten, in Southern California. **For more information on Hal's speaking, writing, and coaching, please visit HalElrod.com.**

RYAN SNOW is a sales leader, business coach, and teacher at heart. With 15 years as a salesperson, teacher, trainer, and business coach, his mission is to help people achieve extraordinary results in life and in sales through personal and professional development. As an early adopter and long-time practitioner of *The Miracle Morning*, Ryan is a firm believer in owning the first few hours of the day for personal and professional growth. Ryan has personally trained hundreds of sales professionals and spoken to thousands about techniques and practices to grow their businesses. Currently, Ryan works as a Team Leader and Business Coach with Keller Williams Realty just outside Boston and manages his own sales team in another office. **If you are interested in speaking with Ryan about sales and accountability coaching, you can find him on Twitter at @Ryan_Snow_RE or email ryansnowcoaching@gmail.com.**

HONORÉE CORDER is the best-selling author of more than a dozen books, including her runaway hit, *Vision to Reality: How Short Term Massive Action Equals Long Term Maximum Results*. Honorée's book has quickly become a must-read for every business professional who desires to go to the next level. For over 15 years, she has passionately served professionals and entrepreneurs as their coach, mentor, and strategic advisor. She empowers others to shed limiting beliefs, dream big, and go for what they truly want. Her mission is to inspire and motivate people to turn their vision and dreams into their real-life reality, sharing a leading-edge process she created for her executive coaching clients. Honorée's results-oriented philosophy and ground-breaking STMA 100-day Coaching Program has been embraced by people in a wide variety of industries and businesses, to rave reviews and exceptional results. **You can find out more about Honorée at HonoreeCorder.com.**

Made in the USA
Lexington, KY
11 November 2015